# MUSIC
# EDUCATION
## IN THE
# CHRISTIAN
# HOME

# MUSIC EDUCATION
## IN THE
# CHRISTIAN HOME

## *The Complete Guide*

## Dr. Mary Ann Froehlich

Wolgemuth & Hyatt, Publishers, Inc.
Brentwood, Tennessee

© 1990 by Mary Ann Froehlich. All rights reserved
Published October 1990. First Edition.
Printed in the United States of America.
97 96 95 94 93 92 91 90   8 7 6 5 4 3 2 1

Unless otherwise noted, all Scripture quotations are from the Holy Bible, New International Version. © 1973, 1978, 1984 International Bible Society. Used by permission of Zondervan Bible Publishers.

Excerpts from The Jerusalem Bible, © 1966 by Darton, Longman & Todd, Ltd. and Doubleday, a division of Bantam Doubleday Dell Publishing Group, Inc. Reprinted by permission.

Wolgemuth & Hyatt, Publishers, Inc.
1749 Mallory Lane, Suite 110
Brentwood, Tennessee 37027

**Library of Congress Cataloging-in-Publication Data**

Froehlich, Mary Ann, 1955—
    Music education in the Christian home : the complete guide / Mary Ann
        Froehlich.
        p.  cm.
    Includes bibliographical references.
    ISBN 1-56121-000-5 (pbk.)
        1. Church music—Instruction and study—Juvenile. 2. Music in the
    home. 3. Church work with children.  I. Title.
    MT88.F75  1990
    780'.7—dc20                                        90-40195
                                                            CIP
                                                            MN

Dedicated to my parents and
the crème de la crème of Suzuki parents:
Christine, Debbie, Georgia, Jana, Patty,
Peggy Sue, and Victoria

# CONTENTS

# ACKNOWLEDGMENTS

Many special thanks to:

- Annette Filice for her music engraving and support.
- Virginia Hiramatsu for her typing and friendship.
- Mary Pride and my friends at Wolgemuth and Hyatt for their expertise and support.
- Peggy Sue Wells for her editing skills and encouragement.
- Donna Clarke, Cecilia Pierotti, and Deborah Casey for sharing their expertise and resources.
- John for his constant love and support, patiently instructing me in computer skills, and teaching me how to minister through music.
- Russ Sorensen for his vision, expertise, and support.
- Darryl Winburne for creating the beautiful time lines.

# *INTERLUDE*

---

Sing to the LORD, all the earth; proclaim his salvation day after day. Declare his glory among the nations, his marvelous deeds among all peoples. (1 Chronicles 16:23–24)

> My heart is ready, God,
>   my heart is ready;
> I mean to sing and play for you,
>   awake, my muse,
> awake, lyre and harp,
>   I mean to wake the Dawn!
>
> Lord, I mean to thank you among the peoples,
>   to play music to you among the nations;
> your love is high as heaven,
>   your faithfulness as the clouds.
> Rise high above the heavens, God,
>   let your glory be over the earth!
>                     (Psalms 57:7–11, TJB)

And all the people went up after him, playing flutes and rejoicing greatly, so that the ground shook with the sound. (1 Kings 1:40)

# 1

## MUSIC EDUCATION IS NOT OPTIONAL FOR GOD'S CHILDREN

*Come, let us praise Yahweh joyfully,*
*acclaiming the Rock of our safety; let us*
*come into his presence with thanksgiving,*
*acclaiming him with music.*

Psalms 95:1–2, TJB

Music making is not optional for God's children. Christian parents have fallen into the secular trap of believing that music education is only one of many opportunities for their children to pursue. Biblically this cannot be supported. As dedicated parents we want our children to have a full range of experiences and skills. If one field does not suit our child, we search for another one. But have you ever seen commanded in Scripture to "play baseball unto the Lord," "enter gymnastics unto the Lord," or "join the Girl Scouts unto the Lord"?

Christian people are certainly called to be involved in secular activities as an outreach and ministry to the community, but music education does not fall in this category. Music making is

*1*

not another "activity." It is a command from God. Over two hundred specific references in Scripture direct us to make music unto the Lord. It is not any more optional than prayer or studying God's Word.

## Music Making Commanded

Scripture clearly teaches that an intimate relationship with God is rooted in music making. It is as much a sign of spiritual health today as it was in Biblical times. If we deprive our children of learning to make music, we are depriving them of a key tool in maintaining a solid relationship with God. Would we expect children to develop a relationship with God throughout a lifetime without giving them a Bible? It is just as serious to deny them the gift and skill of music making. Music is the one gift that God gives to us that we can return to Him and is the essence of a relationship in action.

There is a critical difference between music making unto the Lord and secular lessons and activities pursued to find the child's special niche. The secular activity is for the *child*, for *his* development, while music making is for *God*, for *His* glory and purpose. Dance lessons can be a form of music making to God depending on the orientation of the child and parents and style of dance. There are certainly Biblical examples of celebrating and dancing for God. In fact, a major music education approach of our century, Dalcroze, teaches music skills through responsive movement.

## The Myth of Talent

Our Biblical models were well trained and expert at music making. Are people with no music experience or knowledge who muddle through two hymns on Sunday morning also making music? No, they are tolerating it. We have robbed them of a gift. They are victims of a belief that says that musical skill has something to do with "talent." Accepting that the ability to make music is a "special gift" is the second trap that Christians have fallen into. Music making is a *developed skill*. It is certainly a gift in the sense that every skill we have is given and developed by God, but it is not a "special" skill that belongs only to a chosen few and excludes the majority. The root of that view is human pride.

Realistically, music making is easier for some children than for others. One child may have exceptional eye-hand coordination and make great progress on the piano. Another may have a beautiful voice quality and become the lead singer in the choir. Another has a strong set of lungs and can easily master a difficult wind or brass instrument. The problem starts when we limit music education to those who find it easy. This would be analogous to limiting Bible study to brilliant Greek scholars or prayer to eloquent speakers.

During the 1950s this emphasis on talent was prevalent in our school system and affected the church and society. Music teachers actually used standardized testing to evaluate all students for "musical talent." The teacher did not realize that the test simply revealed whether the students had prior music experience. Only the "talented" ones were placed in music education programs. This crime would be no different from giving a child who has not had a math course a math test or a child who has had no reading experience a reading test and then, upon the failure of those tests, excluding the child from math or reading programs.

The irony of the music aptitude tests was that the students who evidenced home music experience received *more* and the students who did not have home music experience—and most needed the school to provide it—received *none*.

My own mother longed to study piano as a child. When she approached her father about taking music lessons, he replied, "No one in our family has ever had musical talent, and I doubt it starts with you. What you really want to do is exercise your fingers. You will take typing lessons." My mother never received music lessons and has regretted it all her life.

We will discover in the next chapter that music making unto God is inclusive of all believers, never exclusive. The ministry of music begins with music education, to equip God's people with tools. And the music education of our children begins in the home, the most powerful teacher of all Biblical principles. It is the parents' responsibility to oversee each area of their children's education, and music is no exception. This book is designed to guide parents in fulfilling that responsibility and, if they have been denied the gift of music, receiving it themselves. It is never too late to discover God's treasures.

# *INTERLUDE*

And I heard a sound from heaven like the roar of rushing waters and like a loud peal of thunder. The sound I heard was like that of harpists playing their harps. And they sang a new song before the throne and before the four living creatures and the elders. No one could learn the song except the 144,000 who had been redeemed from the earth. (Revelation 14:2–3)

As they began to sing and praise, the LORD set ambushes against the men of Ammon and Moab and Mount Seir who were invading Judah, and they were defeated. (2 Chronicles 20:22)

# 2

# WHY MUSIC MAKING IS NOT OPTIONAL: THE BIBLICAL VIEW

*Hear this, you kings! Listen, you rulers!*
*I will sing to the LORD, I will sing;*
*I will make music to the LORD,*
*the God of Israel.*

Judges 5:3

In highly technological societies such as ours, the arts come to be viewed as frills. They are icing on the cake if time and resources permit—after we focus on what is "important." Observe society's dim view of starving artists and musicians as expendable parasites, not contributors to society. Consider the relegation of the arts to hobby and recreational activities. Look at the rapidly declining arts education programs in our schools. Math and science curricula are required for college prep students while music or art classes are optional or nonexistent.

I was sitting next to a wealthy doctor during one of my husband's business dinners. He told me that his three children were taking Suzuki music lessons and added, "The music les-

7

sons are wonderful. But I wonder if we should be pursuing this. What's the point? What will they ever *do* with it?" The message was if a skill is not tangibly useful to society, then it is unnecessary and a waste of time.

In contrast, historians agree that throughout time the arts have been reliable mirrors of humanity. Humane cultures are marked by their focus on the arts. They prize what is beautiful and pursue it as a priority. Deteriorating cultures, where cruel and barbaric behavior takes hold, are characterized by a disregard for the arts. The destruction of beautiful artwork and musical instruments during war is further proof. Art, the mirror of God's creation and beauty, is not valued in a society where hatred rules.

At the opposite extreme of barbaric culture lies perhaps a worse snare for God's children. In a wealthy, sophisticated society, a knowledge of the arts can be the sign of a cultured individual, contributing to one's image of power and success. The corporate executive who has built a billion-dollar company enjoys attending the symphony, playing Beethoven on his Steinway piano, and collecting fine artwork in the same way he enjoys nouvelle cuisine, good wine, traveling abroad, and having his library filled with classics. The arts are an indication of status.

The Biblical view of the arts, specifically music, is radically different from our culture's view which sometimes seeps into the church. Music making is neither a frill nor a status symbol. It is the core of a right relationship with God. Do you realize that Scripture actually teaches that a healthy spiritual relationship is *impossible* without music?

God reveals five purposes of music in His Word. They stretch far beyond hymn singing on Sunday morning!

1. Music is a tool for corporate worship and obedience.

2. Music is a tool for developing a personal relationship with God.

3. Music is a tool for supporting one another.

4. Music is a tool for victory, our weapon against the enemy.

5. Music is a tool for instruction and witness.

## Tool for Corporate Worship and Obedience

> *Why did you run off secretly and deceive me? Why didn't you tell me, so I could send you away with joy and singing to the music of tambourines and harps?*
>
>                          Genesis 31:27

We are all familiar with the role of music in Sunday morning worship services. Entertaining the congregation is never its purpose. Being entertained and pleasured is a secular *passive* response to art. The purpose of music in worship is to involve us *actively* in an intimate relationship with our God. We are participants, not observers. We become players on the field, not spectators sitting in the bleachers.

Throughout the Old Testament we see a distinct pattern. When God's people return to worshiping and obeying Him after a period of disobedience, they return to music making. The two are synonymous. Upon their return from exile the people of God laid the foundation for the temple and stopped to make music (see Ezra 3:10–11). What construction workers in the business of building churches do you know who stop to sing to God after the foundation is laid? When Nehemiah completed the wall, God's people dedicated it with the organization of two great choirs accompanied by instruments (see Nehemiah 12:27–43). We can trace throughout First and Second Chronicles the repeated disobedience and rededication of God's people. In every instance a return to making music *preceded* obeying and worshiping God (see 2 Chronicles 29:26–30). Making music is evidence of being in right relationship with God.

> Sing joyfully to the LORD, you righteous;
> it is fitting for the upright to praise him.
>
> (Psalms 33:1)

Tied to obedience are thankfulness and praise to God. Biblical music making, through song, dance, and instrument playing, was recognition and celebration of God's goodness. It was a party! The secular world would not think of giving a party without good music. Neither does God! God intended His children to celebrate Him through music.

When David returned home from killing Goliath, the town celebrated with music making (see 1 Samuel 18:6). When the ark of the covenant was brought home, David danced and sang before the Lord (see 2 Samuel 6:16–17). After they passed through the Red Sea and escaped the Egyptians, the Israelites danced and sang on the opposite shore (see Exodus 15). When the prodigal son returned home to his father, they celebrated with music and dancing (see Luke 15:25). An obedient, joyous, and thankful relationship with our God is expressed in music making.

Dance is the expression of joy in Scripture. "Dancing before the Lord" was the response of God's followers to His miracles. Remember how often David danced before the Lord! "As the ark of the LORD was entering the City of David, Michal, daughter of Saul, watched from a window. And when she saw King David leaping and dancing before the LORD, she despised him in her heart" (2 Samuel 6:16).

Greeting a loved one returning home with dancing and singing was an Old Testament tradition. Doesn't it make sense that we should "greet" God and worship Him with the same joyful response? "I will build you up again and you will be rebuilt, O Virgin Israel. Again you will take up your tambourines and go out to dance with the joyful" (Jeremiah 31:4).

Music making in Old Testament times went beyond the congregational singing we practice today. Old Testament music making tied to obedience was serious business. Wherever we see lists of the assignments in the temple, we discover that musicians were assigned second only to the priests. They worked day and night and were exempt from taxes and other duties (see 1 Chronicles 9:33, Ezra 7:24). Old Testament musicians were responsible for the service of the house of God (see Nehemiah 11:22). Contrast this with some present-day churches which view musician positions as necessary afterthoughts. A church may recruit nationwide for a pastor but hope to find someone in the congregation who can supply music.

Musicians were expected to be highly skilled to perform specific duties in the temple, and "choir members" were not exempt from that training: "these who had *learned* to sing to Yahweh were registered with their kinsmen; the total of those so trained was two hundred eighty-eight" (1 Chronicles 25:7, TJB, emphasis added). When Saul searched for a musician, he looked for a harpist who could play *well* (see 1 Samuel 16:17). Serious training was a prerequisite for making music to God as evidenced by the psalmist:

> Give thanks to Yahweh on the lyre,
> play to him on the ten-string harp;
> sing a new song in his honor,
> play with *all your skill* as you acclaim him!
>       (Psalms 33:2–3, TJB, emphasis added)

## Tool for a Personal
## Relationship with God

> *Rejoice in the* LORD *and be glad,*
> *you righteous;*
> *sing, all you who are upright*
> *in heart!*
>       Psalms 32:11

Music making is as much a part of our individual relationship with God as it is a tool for our group relationship as a church body. It is rare to find a reference in Scripture where praising God and communicating through prayer are not linked with music making. The Psalms, the music of Scripture, are our primary example.

It is no surprise that when people most need comfort, they turn to the Psalms. Hearts filled with gratefulness to God look to the Psalms to express their joy. James specifically tells us if we are happy, we should sing praises to God (see James 5:13). Scripture is clear on this point: God gave us the gift of music to respond to Him. He has given us a new song:

> He has put a new song in my mouth
>   a song of praise to our God.
>
>                    (Psalms 40:3a, TJB)

> You have turned my mourning into dancing,
> you have stripped off my sackcloth and
>   wrapped me in gladness;
> and now my heart, silent no longer,
>   will play you music;
> Yahweh, my God, I will praise you for ever.
>                    (Psalms 30:11–12, TJB)

We are to trust God, rely on God, and thank Him through song:

> But I for my part rely on your love, Yahweh;
> let my heart rejoice in your saving help.
> Let me sing to Yahweh for the goodness
>   he has shown me.
>                    (Psalms 13:5, TJB)

Notice that prayer and song are an interchangeable communication with God:

> In the daytime may Yahweh
>   command his love to come,
> and by night may his song be on my lips,
>   a prayer to the God of my life!
>                    (Psalms 42:8, TJB)

So what shall I do? I will pray with my spirit, but I will also pray with my mind; I will sing with my spirit, but I will also sing with my mind. (1 Corinthians 14:15)

We cannot escape the fact that music making is an integral part of our active, communicating relationship with God. The psalmist goes so far as to *promise* to play and sing to God. Music making is our *commitment* to praise Him. It is our commanded response:

> I promise I will thank you on the lyre,
>    my ever-faithful God,
> I will play the harp in your honor,
>    Holy One of Israel.
> My lips shall sing for joy as I play to you,
>    and this soul of mine which you have redeemed.
>
> (Psalms 71:22–23, TJB)

> Then will I ever sing praise to your name
>    and fulfill my vows day after day.
>
> (Psalms 61:8)

## Tool for Supporting One Another

Realizing that music making is key to our personal relationship with God helps us understand why it is an effective way to support our brethren. We observe in Ephesians 5:19–20 that we are to "speak *to one another* with psalms, hymns and spiritual songs. Sing and make music in your heart to the Lord, always giving thanks to God the Father for everything, in the name of our Lord Jesus Christ" (emphasis added).

There is an intimate link between (1) the indwelling of Christ in believers, (2) song, and (3) supporting one another, the end result being (4) thankfulness and celebration:

> Let the word of Christ dwell in you richly as you teach and admonish one another with all wisdom, and as you sing psalms, hymns and spiritual songs with gratitude in your hearts to God. And whatever you do, whether in word or

deed, do it all in the name of the Lord Jesus, giving thanks to God the Father through him. (Colossians 3:16–17)

Music making and the spiritual growth process are inseparable.

Church music ministry focuses on speaking to one another in song on Sunday morning with the role of music minister being to prepare for those worship experiences. The task should continue from here. We are instructed to sing to the Lord in our hearts, to make music a way of life. We should each be "music ministers."

Many dedicated music ministers develop comprehensive music and worship programs for their fellowships but are misunderstood by congregation members. Music ministers cannot do their jobs alone anymore than pastors can shepherd their congregations alone. They equip the saints to minister alongside them. The church and home need to become partners in the ministry of music.

Further study in chapter 6 will reveal how God provided music to be daily food and comfort for those experiencing trial and suffering. "Singing songs to a sorrowing heart" is God's prescription for treating wounds (see Proverbs 25:20). Music making is a tool for victory in times of distress.

God sets the lonely in families, he leads forth the prisoners with singing; but the rebellious live in a sun-scorched land. (Psalms 68:6)

## Tool for Victory

*And now my head is held high*
*over the enemies who surround me,*
*in his tent I will offer*
*exultant sacrifice.*
*I will sing, I will play for Yahweh!*
Psalms 27:6, TJB

Biblical music making was a weapon against our spiritual enemy and a tool toward assuring victory.

Jesus understood the power of music in facing trial. The last event that He and His disciples shared before leaving for the Mount of Olives was the singing of psalms together (see Matthew 26:30). Paul and Silas sang hymns of praise with their feet in prison stocks (see Acts 16:25). Saul used music making in his battle with depression (see 1 Samuel 16:23). Old Testament armies sometimes sent the choir ahead of them as they faced the enemy (see 2 Chronicles 20:21). Cast into the fiery furnace, Daniel's friends, Shadrach, Meshach, and Abednego sang songs of praise to God and not a hair on their heads was singed (see Daniel 3:51–90). When the evil spirit came upon Saul to harm David, David was found playing the harp and remained safe (see 1 Samuel 18:10).

Scripture clearly teaches that music making to God is *powerful*. Music is that unbreakable, tangible link with God. Music is inseparable from His presence (see Revelation 14:2–3). We will unceasingly praise God in song and be surrounded by music in our heavenly home. The book of Revelation reveals that God will remove music as a further punishment to His enemies on the final day of judgment (see 18:22).

Is it any surprise that Scripture set to music is easy to remember? Is it any wonder we tell young children to sing when they are afraid? I tell the children in my church choir to sing to God in times of worry, fear, or trouble. We can imagine our enemy putting his hands over his ears and screaming, "No! Don't sing to God! I can't stand it!" as he runs away from us. Music is the unconquerable weapon of God's presence that we carry with us.

> You are my hiding place;
>     you will protect me from trouble
>     and surround me with songs of deliverance.
>
> (Psalms 32:7)

> Because you are my help,
>     I sing in the shadow of your wings.
>
> (Psalms 63:7)

A missionary recently recounted, "We decided to counter the cannibals by singing hymns. We began with 'Anywhere with Jesus I can safely go,' and ended with 'There is power in the blood.' Suddenly they ceased their crazed orgy, and to the surprise of our black guide, they ran away, leaving us in safety. Apparently they could not bear to hear the name of Jesus and the mention of His redeeming blood." These cannibals were reached for Christ. Later the same missionary wrote, "A church of 400 Christians has been established here. Today they partook of the Lord's Supper, singing not in terror, but with shining faces, 'What can wash away my sin? Nothing but the blood of Jesus.' "*

## Tool for Instruction and Witness

*Sing to the LORD, for he has done*
*glorious things; let this be known*
*to all the world.*

Isaiah 12:5

God intended our music making to instruct others and provide a witness to His truth. It is an integral part of Christian education and evangelism. We are learning that music permeates every task of the church.

God often instructed the Israelites through song. The "Song of Moses" is the most dramatic example. Moses was facing death soon and bringing his final messages to the people. Note the introduction:

"Now write down for yourselves this song and teach it to the Israelites and have them sing it, so that it may be a witness for me against them. When I have brought them into the land flowing with milk and honey, the land I promised on oath to their forefathers, and when they eat their fill and thrive, they will turn to other gods and worship them, rejecting me and

---

* Clark, David. Sermon: Delivered in the First Baptist Church, Benecia, California, 8 November 1987.

breaking my covenant. And when many disasters and difficulties come upon them, this song will testify against them, because it will not be forgotten by their descendants. I know what they are disposed to do, even before I bring them into the land I promised them on oath." So Moses wrote down this song that day and taught it to the Israelites. (Deuteronomy 31:19–22)

The accepted educational fact that "song reinforces learning" has Biblical roots. The psalmist says, "I will declare your name to my brothers; in the congregation I will praise you" (Psalms 22:22).

Spiritual teaching through music was intended for nonbelievers as well as believers. When Paul and Silas were singing hymns to God in prison, *the other prisoners were listening to them* (see Acts 16:25). Observe the commands to testify to God's salvation through song:

> I will sing of the Lord's great love forever;
>> with my mouth I will make your faithfulness known
>>> through all generations.
>
> (Psalms 89:1)

> Sing to him, sing praise to him;
>> tell of all his wonderful acts.
>
> (Psalms 105:2)

> May my tongue sing of your word,
>> for all your commands are righteous.
>
> (Psalms 119:172)

God delights in responding to our music making. The Israelites ". . . raised their voices in praise to the LORD and sang: 'He is good; his love endures forever.' Then the temple of the LORD was filled with a cloud" (2 Chronicles 5:13). God was present in their music making. The hand of the Lord came upon Elisha *while* the harpist was playing (see 2 Kings 3:15). God's Spirit came upon Saul through a group of prophets playing instruments (see 1 Samuel 10:5). God comes to us in music. He even sings back to us!

> The LORD your God is with you, he is mighty to save. He will take great delight in you, he will quiet you with his love, he will rejoice over you with singing. (Zephaniah 3:17)

Every revival of faith, from the work of Martin Luther to John and Charles Wesley to the Great Awakening to the American Pentecostal revival, has included a return to fresh, creative, and joy-filled music making.

If our Biblical characters could be with us today, I am sure that they would ask, baffled, how we hold prayer meetings, congregational meetings, deacon meetings, or any meeting where God's people gather without music making. No wonder *living* churches are recognized by their emphasis on music, prayer, and celebration to God, the evidence of an *active* relationship *with* God. *Dying* churches are marked by information, announcements, and such *about* God. In all fairness, perhaps the lack of music is not as much an indication of spirituality as it is a product of inadequate music education.

Yet music education is not the ultimate answer. All the musical expertise in the world does not cure a hardened heart against God. Sometimes those who sing the most off pitch, sing with the brightest smiles and most joyous love for their Lord.

In review:

1. Music making evidences:

    a. an active relationship of open communication with God.

    b. a right relationship of trust, obedience, and thankfulness.

    c. our individual as well as group response.

    d. a joyful desire to worship and greet Him.

2. Music making to God incorporates song, dance, and instrument playing. We are commanded to celebrate Him through song.

3. Biblical music makers were highly skilled. They pursued training as a priority. Mediocrity was not acceptable.

4. We are to use music in our daily lives to encourage and comfort one another.

5. Music making is inseparable from God's presence. It is a powerful tool against our spiritual enemy.

6. Music making instructs believers and witnesses to nonbelievers.

7. God delights in responding to our music making. He comes to us in music.*

---

* You will find in the appendixes a listing of all the Biblical references on music and dance.

# *INTERLUDE*

Acclaim God, all the earth,
play music to the glory of his name,
glorify him with your praises,
say to God, "What dread you inspire!"

Your achievements are the measure of your power.
Your enemies cringe in your presence;
all the earth bows down to you,
playing music for you, playing in honor
    of your name.

(Psalms 66:1–4, TJB)

The men did the work faithfully. Over them to direct them were Jahath and Obadiah, Levites descended from Merari, and Zechariah and Meshullam, descended from Kohath. The Levites—all who were skilled in playing musical instruments. (2 Chronicles 34:12)

# 3

## MUSIC MINISTRY BEGINS WITH MUSIC EDUCATION

*Kenaniah the head Levite was in charge of
the singing; that was his responsibility
because he was skillful at it.*

1 Chronicles 15:22

**M**usic making to God is a learning process. God deserves our best gifts in every area of life, and musical gifts are no exception. Yet the world's standards do not apply. The accomplished operatic soprano's gift is not *better* than the four-year-old's simple bedtime song. They are both offering their best, and each gift is treasured by God.

We have learned that Biblical music making was skillful. Singing, playing instruments, movement, and composing are complex skills that require training. Music ministry begins with music education. Music education is not pageantry. It is not performance. Those experiences, which my own children love, can be a wonderful by-product of music education, but music making does not originate there.

Music education equips people with skills they are learning to use independently. Independent mastery is the goal of all education. Mature believers study the Bible and pray to God apart from the guidance of their church leaders. Never limited to Sundays, those activities contribute daily to our individual relationships with God. Music making was intended for that same purpose.

Up until the last century, the church and home were the primary centers of music education in society. Before the nineteenth century, musicians were employed in either the church or the court of royalty. Monasteries were the home of music education during the Middle Ages. In the Renaissance the Reformation brought sacred music and the Bible out of the monasteries to the people in their own languages and in their own homes.

Sacred music remained a significant part of composers' contributions for centuries. J. S. Bach, a godly man and perhaps the most famous church musician, received his training at home from his family. Bach passed his skills on to his own children, most notably Carl Philipp Emanuel Bach and Johann Christian Bach. The Bach family resembled a chain, passing their musical heritage on through the generations. Mozart's training was also rooted in the home under his father's instruction. Throughout history, shared family music experiences and home chamber concerts were a natural part of family life.

In our own country, up until the 1800s, it was the church's role to provide music education. In 1832 Lowell Mason, the well-known church musician, hymn composer, and music educator, founded the private Boston Academy of Music. His dedicated efforts brought music education for children into the public school system in Boston in 1838, and eventually music programs spread through schools nationwide.

As music curricula became more established in public schools and private academies, the church and home eventually abdicated their positions as music educators. Now that many public schools are tragically losing their music education programs to financial cutbacks, it is encouraging to see churches and families assuming that responsibility once more.

Equal to that responsibility is the task of becoming knowledgeable about music education. That task will be our focus for the remainder of this book.

## Current Music Education Methods

Long gone are the days of amateur music teachers instructing young students to count ledger lines on the staff as their first music learning experiences. Today music education is a complex, researched field with multiple specializations. It is challenge enough for professional music educators, much less parents, to keep up with current developments.

Four major music education methods of our day that are especially relevant for young children are Kodály, Dalcroze, Orff-Schulwerk, and Suzuki. An introduction to each follows.

## The Kodály Method

Zoltán Kodály (1882-1967) developed in the Hungarian schools a comprehensive approach to music education, which is recognized worldwide as the Kodály Method.

It is based on the following principles:

1. Kodály believed that *all* people can become musically literate as they are language literate. Reading and writing music should be as natural for children as reading and writing their native language. Kodály viewed music as a core subject to be taught daily in the classroom on a level with academic subjects. (Reading specialists have learned in the past decade that rhythm is a key factor in teaching reading.)

2. The natural activity of singing is the basis for teaching musicianship, hence the term "choral musicianship." The singing process is accessible to all and immediately inter-

nalized. Song materials should come from the folk song repertoire of the child's own culture.

3. To be most effective, music education must begin with the very young child.

4. Children should be exposed to the highest quality in music from folk songs to serious art music. Aesthetic sensitivity is developed in people. We are not simply born with a discerning taste for good art.

Kodály based his systematic method on the natural progression of developmental skills in children. For example, all children throughout the world sing their earliest songs on the minor third interval in duple rhythm. What child does not tease others with this?

Na-ni  Na-ni  Na - ni,    Can't catch— me! ——

Note our first folk songs:

Rain, rain,   go  a - way    Ring a-round the ros - ey

As children grow, they naturally include more intervals of the scale and more complex rhythms in their song literature. Kodály developed a carefully sequenced approach which taught children musical skills in the order that they were ready for them. He incorporated movement and folk dance as an extension of singing.

Kodály employed an established sight-singing tool, Sol-fa, to teach music reading. Observe this scale (to be applied in any key) with Sol-fa designations:

Children read music, singing these syllables:

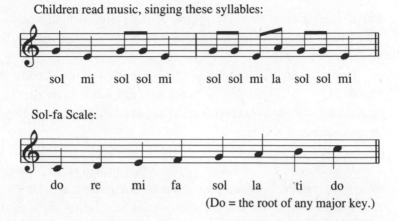

sol   mi   sol sol mi      sol sol mi la   sol sol mi

Sol-fa Scale:

do      re      mi      fa      sol      la      ti      do
(Do = the root of any major key.)

It is a well-known fact that children in Hungarian schools sight-sing music far more expertly than most college music majors in our own country! It is as natural to them as reading books.

Kodály combined the Sol-fa system with hand signals, which originated with John Curwen in England. Each Sol-fa syllable corresponds with a specific hand signal that reinforces tonal memory.

Rhythmic durations are also assigned syllabic patterns. For example:

♩ ta,      ♩♩ ti - ti

Rhythms are initially taught without the actual notes. For example:

♫ = ⊓

Developing musical memory and inner hearing are other vital aspects of the Kodály method. Children are taught to think songs internally (to "sing in their heads"). Children in Hungarian school settings do not begin instrument study until they have mastered Kodály choral skills. The rationale is "if you can't sing it (know it internally), you can't play it."

## The Dalcroze Method

What the singing voice is to the Kodály method, the natural movement responses of the human body to rhythm are to the Dalcroze method.

Emile Jaques-Dalcroze (1865-1950) viewed movement as the method for internalizing musicianship skills. His method, termed *eurhythmics,* had an impact on music education, as well as on dance and therapy.

While he was a professor at the Conservatory of Music in Geneva, Dalcroze found that his students, though exceptionally advanced on their instruments, could not master the simplest rhythm problems. He further discovered that while they could not play in tempo, his pupils could easily walk in tempo. The students could not *feel* the flow of a musical phrase while playing their instruments, yet their muscles tensed at the height of the musical phrase and relaxed at the end. Although natural music making was *in* their bodies, it wasn't transferring to their playing.

As a result, Dalcroze developed an individual system of rhythmic movement exercises based on the following principles:

1. Rhythm is the basic element of all music.

2. Rhythm is motion. All rhythms in music have their roots in the natural rhythm of the human body and can be experienced in movement.

3. Our bodies are our first instruments. We cannot play music that we cannot first feel through movement.

Eurhythmics is *not* to be confused with dance. Children engaged in creative dance activities are *not* experiencing the Dalcroze method. Eurhythmics focuses on our kinesthetic sense, that link between experiential movement and cognitive processing. Today therapists and educators are well aware of the role of the kinesthetic sense in treating clients and students.

Dalcroze's movement repertoire consists of movements in place and movements in space* (see table 1). Different combinations of movements comprise the exercises as the students respond to musical changes. The preparation for the movement and relaxation after the movement is just as important rhythmically as the action itself.

| Table 1: Movement Vocabulary | |
| --- | --- |
| **Movements in Place** | **Movements in Space** |
| Clapping | Walking |
| Swinging | Running |
| Turning | Crawling |
| Conducting | Leaping |
| Bending | Sliding |
| Swaying | Galloping |
| Speaking | Skipping |
| Singing | |

The Dalcroze teacher improvises music at the piano, combining different elements of rhythm and including "surprises" for the students to respond to. Exercises proceed from simple walking and clapping for the youngest students to the most complex rhythmic problems for advanced students.

Eurhythmics is the hallmark of the Dalcroze method, because it was his creation, but the method actually consists of three parts:

1. Rhythmic movement.

2. Solfège singing (similar to the Sol-fa singing used in the Kodály method). The development of inner hearing and memory is key.

---

* Choksy, et al., *Teaching Music in the 20th Century* (Englewood Cliffs, NJ: Prentice-Hall, 1986), 37.

3. Improvisation. Through movement, speech, song, and instruments, students are expected to create spontaneously and play at music making as opposed to being mechanically tied to written notes on the page. Dalcroze's goal was for his students to experience the same freedom on their advanced instruments that they experienced in movement.

Dalcroze viewed musicianship as the integration of inner hearing, inner muscular response, and creative expression. Attending to our kinesthetic sense is a learned process.

## The Orff-Schulwerk Method

Orff-Schulwerk was developed by the German-born composer, Carl Orff (1895–1982). Orff never set out to develop one of the most innovative music education approaches of our century. His initial dream was to integrate music and dance effectively for the theater. His work with Dorothea Günther, trainer of dancers and gymnasts, eventually evolved into his *Schulwerk,* his school work.

Orff observed that children experience music, movement, speech (songs, chants) simultaneously in their play, not separately. This natural process of music making he termed "elemental." Orff believed children should be taught music as they naturally experience it, through an integration of music, speech, movement, and childhood chants.

Orff-Schulwerk begins with the person and the creative *process,* not a desired musical *product.* Orff experience is spontaneous and unplanned. The children create it. Like Dalcroze, Orff believed rhythm was central to music making and should be developed in early childhood. The process begins with materials of the child's world, such as the rhythm of his or her own name.

Orff-Schulwerk is rooted in exploration and creative experience. It is a method of play, which we all know to be the child's work. Orff students explore space through movement, sound through speech, song, and instruments, and patterns of music ("form"). They begin by imitating the Orff leader and move to improvising their own creations. Orff students work as a community; they are an ensemble.

Unique to the Orff-Schulwerk method are the Orff instruments, influenced by Orff's exposure to African and Indonesian music. The Orff instrumentarium is easily accessible to children's abilities and offers a variety of timbres and textures including cymbals, drums, glockenspiels, metallophones, recorders, strings, and other folk rhythm instruments. Children progress from making music with their bodies (snapping, *patschen,** clapping, stamping) to improvising music on complex instruments. Orchestral instruments are also used.

Musical elements in the beginning Orff-Schulwerk process are the use of:

1. The pentatonic mode. (This scale without the fourth and seventh tones is the source of all childhood folk songs. The minor third is universally central to children's songs.)

1    2    3    5    6

2. Ostinato patterns (patterns that repeat) and the development of motives.

3. Simple forms, e.g., canon, rondo.

4. Children's materials/songs from their own culture.

5. Creative dramatics, poetry, and story literature to develop music dramas at the child's level.

Advanced Orff-Schulwerk incorporates complex harmonies, mixed meters, modes, music forms (e.g., theme and variations,

---

* *Patschen* is thigh slapping.

music drama), and dance forms, leading students to a mastery of improvisatory composition skills.

Carl Orff and Gunild Keetman composed *Music for Children,* five volumes of Orff-style orchestrations for instructing children. These have been adapted for use in other cultures. Children are taught to read music notation when it is relevant. It is seen as a tool for communication. Students learn to write what they compose to share with others in the ensemble. Memorizing remains the key; students are not tied to written notes on the page.

Orff-Schulwerk is that unique magical process that taps every creative facet of our beings. It has influenced music therapy, benefiting exceptional clients, as well as music education. Orff-Schulwerk is a method of experimentation leading to complex improvisations. It can be as simple as a developmentally disabled child playing the rhythm of his name on a drum or a group of emotionally disturbed adolescents expressing their emotions through creating an Orff composition. Or it can be as involved as a group of adults spontaneously enacting the entire Passion and Resurrection narrative for Easter through song, speech, movement, and instruments. The creative possibilities are endless.

## The Suzuki Method

The Suzuki method is founded on the mother tongue concept. Dr. Shinichi Suzuki (1898–) observed that all children immersed in their language since birth, learn to speak the native tongue expertly. Suzuki spent his life demonstrating that similar immersion in a musical home environment develops an equal fluency in music. Suzuki has exposed the myth of "talent." Talent is instead an ability that can be developed in the proper environment, hence the terms ability development, or talent education, method.

Suzuki music making is a product of listening and experience, not of matching notes on a page. Pieces are taught by imitation. Suzuki felt that teaching a child to read music before the child can make it is analogous to teaching a child to read before he can speak. Symbols cannot be associated with a process one has never experienced. Music reading should be postponed until after the child's musical skills are established.

Born in Nagoya, Japan, Suzuki grew up as the son of a violin maker in a musical family. He began seriously studying the violin at age seventeen and progressed rapidly. At age twenty-three he went to Germany to study with Karl Klinger and was greatly influenced by Western music and culture. He began working with small children and developing his philosophy in 1931. Prompted by his desire to bring healing to children devastated in World War II, Suzuki formally opened the Matsumoto Talent Education School in 1945. The school grew rapidly, is flourishing today, and offers musical instruction in various instruments, art, calligraphy, English, gymnastics, and math, all employing the Suzuki approach.

Suzuki values the human potential of any individual and believes that there are no failures. Though it is never too late to begin the Suzuki process, the method is rooted in starting children as early as possible. Suzuki developed a listening environment program for infants. Children begin formal individual and group music lessons on an instrument during the preschool years and continue the process as a way of life. Suzuki followers emphasize it is not a music education method but an approach to living.

Due to the success of the talent education method, there exist many five-year-old Suzuki students playing Mozart piano sonatas and Vivaldi violin concertos. Though his critics have charged Suzuki with turning out robot prodigies, close examination of the Suzuki method discloses this was never his intention. Suzuki's conviction is that a musical life is an enriched, full, and happier life. Suzuki is focused on comprehensive education of the human potential and the well-being of the whole child. Two well-known statements by Suzuki embody his philosophy:

"Where love is deep, much can be accomplished" * and "Character first, ability second." † He believes a highly developed musical intellect and sensitivity will transfer to all areas of life. As a prime example, Suzuki cited Einstein who said his idea of relativity formed at age sixteen as the direct result of Einstein's own musical perception and experience.

The practical techniques of the Suzuki method are:

1. Music education begins at birth. Children are exposed daily to high quality music, cultural folk songs as well as serious art music, in their environment.

2. Students begin actual study on an instrument during the preschool years. It is play. They learn by imitating the teacher and daily listening to recordings of high quality songs they are learning to play. Beginning students learn childhood folk songs. Children's ears are their best teachers. They are not simply imitating the notes, but how the notes are played. The Suzuki repertoire is a carefully sequenced set of books, with corresponding recordings, adapted for each instrument. Daily listening accelerates the learning process and most closely parallels the way we learn our native tongues.

   Instruments using the Suzuki approach today are the cello, flute, harp, piano, viola, and violin. Small scale cellos, violas, and violins, flutes with curved mouthpieces, and troubadour harps are available for young children. Piano students play normal-size pianos and use a footstool box for their feet.‡

3. The Suzuki method starts with life experience and returns to it. Experiences familiar to the student are used to teach

---

* S. Suzuki, *Where Love Is Deep,* trans. Kyoka Seldon (St. Louis, MO: Talent Education Journal, 1982).

† S. Suzuki, *Nurtured by Love,* trans. Waltraud Suzuki (Smithtown, NY: Exposition, 1973).

‡ The Suzuki method for voice is being developed by the Harnes-Selway Creative Arts Program.

musical principles, and the accomplishment transfers to other skill areas. For example, the first pieces learned in *Suzuki Book I* for all instruments are the "Twinkle, Twinkle, Little Star Variations." The rhythmic variations on this familiar folk song encompass all basic aspects of technique and musicality and are the foundation of the method. The rhythms are first learned by saying speech patterns, clapping, moving, and playing them on rhythm instruments; finally they are transferred to the studied instrument. Speech patterns of food names are often used because food is common to everyone's experience. For example,

♫♫ ♪♪   = Pepperoni Pizza

4. The greatest criticism of the Suzuki method has been that Suzuki students do not learn to read music until it is too late. Suzuki never intended to produce nonreaders. He wanted students to start early enough to have had those musical experiences before learning to read music at the traditional age. Supplementary reading methods are encouraged at the proper level. The attack that Suzuki students can't read is simply invalid and evidences a teacher's failure to be thorough.

5. Ability breeds ability. Each Suzuki piece and technique builds upon previous pieces. The method moves the child in small steps that can be easily mastered. Students set their own pace.

6. Constant repetition is the key to mastery. Previous pieces in the Suzuki books are consistently reviewed. Suzuki students know their repertoire so well that written music is not needed and performance for others is natural and joyous. For example, upon completion of *Suzuki Book I,* students give a "Book I Recital," in which they play their entire repertoire of nineteen pieces.

7. The Suzuki method focuses on the total well-being and self-esteem of children, not their musical product. The Suzuki environment is joyful and safe. The student is always affirmed for what is done right, never criticized for mistakes. Suzuki lessons are one success experience after another.

8. The Suzuki method is a family method. The parent is the home teacher. The parent attends all lessons, takes notes, and receives instruction. If not already a musician, the parent will become one through working with the child daily at home! The Suzuki method teaches that it is never too early or too late to learn.

9. Traditional instrumental music lessons tend to isolate students from their peers or employ competitions and contests to "motivate" them. Suzuki students do not "take lessons"; they are part of a Suzuki program that is a group experience. They have private sessions with their Suzuki teacher and parent weekly and attend group lessons to make music with other students. An attitude of cooperation and helping one another to learn (versus competition) is taught. A Suzuki program is a supportive community.

10. The Suzuki method is effective with all ages and all abilities. It has been employed with toddlers through aging adults. The method has successfully helped mentally and physically limited children.

## Other Methods

In our century other methods and music education programs certainly exist—for example, the Manhattanville Music Curriculum Program, Comprehensive Musicianship, and the Young Composers Project. But since they are more suited to classroom use for older students, we will simply mention them. Their goals are

no different from those of the four methods described—to develop well-rounded experiential musicians.

In contrast to Dalcroze, Kodály, Orff-Schulwerk or Suzuki,
what are "traditional" methods? "Traditional" is not actually a
method; it is a catchall term. It refers to viewing music education as teaching music reading. Since traditional music teachers
do not accept students until they are old enough to read the
printed word, students begin reading music at their first lesson.
Music lessons are actually "music reading" lessons using the
chosen instrument as the tool.

It is critical that parents understand the following point:
When educators and psychologists adamantly oppose music education for the young child, they oppose pushing the child into
traditional methods before the child is ready. Today's music
educators couldn't agree more! However, most educators and
psychologists are unfamiliar with the work of Kodály, Dalcroze,
Orff-Schulwerk, and Suzuki, and with their focus on music *experience* for the young child. These educational experts would
never deny the importance of music experiences in the young
child's life! Music education is music experience and play for
young children.

Today Kodály, Dalcroze, Orff-Schulwerk, and Suzuki teachers lean away from traditional methods. But in all fairness, we
professional music educators were probably all trained by traditional teachers—and well trained, at that. Perhaps, as is true for
me, today's educators also enjoyed singing, listening to recordings, and dance lessons in early childhood. Music experience remains the key.


## Which Method Is Best for Your Child?

The answer to this question is that no one method is "better."
Kodály, Dalcroze, Orff-Schulwerk, and Suzuki are all outstanding, effective, and thorough music education methods, tapping

all areas of child development. A child would be privileged to experience any one of them.

Though their techniques vary, the philosophies of the four methods are similar. Their common principles offer a guide to effective music education:

- Children should have music experiences as young as possible. All people can become as musically literate as they are language literate. "Talent" is a myth.

- Through experience, singing, movement, and listening, children should internalize musicianship skills before moving on to apply them to instrument study.

- Music *experience* must precede music reading. Inner hearing of what one will play must precede actually playing it.

- Children should be exposed to the highest quality music materials, from the folk songs of their culture through serious art music.

- Comprehensive (well-rounded) musicianship is the goal. Developing musical sensitivity and understanding the nuances of phrasing, dynamics, and so on, are inherent in each method.

- A cooperative spirit of ensemble music making is encouraged. Competition has no place.

- Children should be taught music in the way they naturally experience it as they develop, through movement, listening, chant/song, and instrument experimentation. Pedagogical material should come from the child's own world.

- Rhythm is the source of all music experience. Melody grows out of rhythm.

- The music experience is a process, the goal being the total well-being of the student. The goal is never a musical *product,* or producing a "prodigy" or a professional musician. An appreciation for music develops finer human beings. Music making is a gift of lifetime enjoyment.

In line with our eclectic American culture, music educators sometimes try to combine the four methods to obtain the "best of all worlds." Experts in each method agree that the resulting mishmash waters the method down to no value. It would be better for students to experience one method thoroughly or the four methods separately over time for the full impact of each. For example, students could study Orff-Schulwerk one year and Kodály another year. Suzuki students could study Dalcroze during a summer program. The combinations will necessarily depend on the offerings parents find in their area. The Suzuki method is effective when combined with other methods because it focuses on instrument mastery. Kodály, Dalcroze, and Orff-Schulwerk each develop comprehensive musicianship while Suzuki offers specialization on a specific instrument.

As a Suzuki teacher and Orff-Schulwerk-trained music therapist, I agree that mishmash should be avoided. Yet music educators should know about each method. Kodály, Dalcroze, and Orff certainly learned from each other. Ideally, we can become fully trained and primarily focus on one method while incorporating strengths of the other methods when relevant. This view is in response to the reality that most families do not have access, logistically or financially, to programs featuring each of these methods. Suzuki students should learn Solfège and have movement experiences; Kodály students should be encouraged to improvise and engage in instrument play; and Dalcroze and Orff-Schulwerk students should have daily listening programs.

In my Suzuki-Orff group classes, for example, students enjoy creating spontaneous Orff play as well as Orff ensemble orchestrations on the Suzuki literature that they play. Parents who play instruments bring them to class and join in the music making. All siblings and parents can sing and play rhythm instruments. Orff ensembles are also effective when incorporated into the yearly recital. They create an atmosphere of celebration and joy for everyone involved. The key is to integrate methods only when integration strengthens each approach, never when blending detracts from both.

## Church Application

*Clap your hands, all you peoples,*
*acclaim God with shouts of joy.*
                              Psalms 47:1, TLB

Scripture suggests that God intended music experiences to be integrated and in keeping with our development as He created us. Music is as important to the community as it is to our growth as individuals. It should be obvious that the discoveries of music education research are in line with Biblical principles.

Today many children's music ministers are taking their primary role as music educators seriously, pursuing training in Kodály, Dalcroze, Orff-Schulwerk, or Suzuki and applying these techniques in church choral programs. The focus is shifting from church pageantry to serious music education, which enriches the musical praise to God in worship services. This is a far cry from a music program with the sole purpose of providing the holiday musical pageant with glorious costumes.

With its focus on ensemble singing, use of Sol-fa, teaching of rhythms, and training of musical memory, Kodály has obvious applications for the church choir. Orff-Schulwerk has become popular in churches for its use of instruments with song and speech, coupled with playful exploration and composition. When space allows, Dalcroze or Orff-Schulwerk movement activities are valuable.

Choral pieces scored with Orff instrumentation are excellent additions to the literature but are not to be confused with the Orff-Schulwerk process. That process originates with the children. A true Orff experience might begin with a Scripture verse. The leader would help the children create a chant inspired by it. Then they would add harmonies with voice and instrumentation, movement and dramatics. Orff is an improvised creation.

Even the Suzuki method has important contributions for the church class. In leading a Suzuki-Orff preschool program in our church, I applied the following Suzuki principles:

1. The parent was the home teacher. Parents were required to:
   a. Attend an introductory lecture on the "myth of talent," current music education methods, and their role as home teachers.
   b. Attend the class on a rotation basis to assist the leader and learn the music activities to implement them at home.
2. Children listened to quality music in their homes daily, including music sung in class. Parents were given a list of resources.
3. The class focused on:
   a. Providing musical experiences for young children.
   b. Using high quality folk and spiritual songs coupled with Twinkle rhythm patterns. Folk songs and *Suzuki Book I* pieces were used with a spiritual adaptation of the lyrics.
   c. Building a song repertoire through consistent review.

The program worked so well that our adult choir adopted the Suzuki listening philosophy. Each member received a tape of the year's more difficult works with his or her part emphasized. Choir members learned their parts in record time!

Developing church choral programs into graded comprehensive music education classes provides a much needed service and ministry to the community, especially if quality music education programs are scarce. The church can serve its own members and become a "community music school" as well.

# *INTERLUDE*

---

Teach us to count how few days we have
and so gain wisdom of heart.
Relent, Yahweh! How much longer do we have?
Take pity on your servants!

Let us wake in the morning filled with your love
and sing and be happy all our days.
(Psalms 90:12–14, TJB)

So all Israel brought up the ark of the covenant of the LORD with shouts, with the sounding of rams' horns and trumpets, and of cymbals, and the playing of lyres and harps. (1 Chronicles 15:28)

# 4

## LISTENING: THE CORE OF THE MUSIC EDUCATION PROGRAM

*My song is about kindness and justice;*
*Yahweh, I sing it to you.*

Psalms 101:1, TJB

Listening to high quality music is the core of any music education program. A developing musician who has never heard beautiful music as a model cannot make it, any more than an artist who has never seen a beautiful painting can create, or a dancer who has never attended the ballet can dance. One cannot learn *about* the arts; they must be *experienced* with our God-given senses. Music is an *aural* art and must be learned that way.

Children should be exposed to a variety of music styles. Most parents are comfortable in the world of folk songs, rock, sometimes jazz, and other mediums of our day, but are lost when it comes to the world of serious art music ("Classicalal" music). There is a good reason that this is overwhelming; it requires a knowledge of western music history spanning eight centuries!

"Classical" music is the first misnomer; it refers only to music from the Classical period of the eighteenth century, which limits listening primarily to Mozart and Haydn. There are actually six periods of music corresponding to those periods of history:

| | |
|---|---|
| Medieval | Middle Ages–14th century |
| Renaissance | 15th–16th century |
| Baroque | 17th century |
| Classic | 18th century |
| Romantic | 19th century |
| Twentieth Century | 20th century |

The following introduction will help parents to develop a listening program for their children. You can borrow recordings from the local library or buy them for your own lifetime library. For difficult-to-find recordings, try visiting your nearest university music library.

In addition, students should attend live events such as concerts, ballets, and operas. Expose them to contemporary music forms. Their skills will only be well-rounded if their ears are well-rounded.

The listed works are a starting point. They are representative, not exhaustive and present a music history overview.

## Medieval

- Gregorian chant in the church

- Monophonic secular songs: Troubadour/trouvère songs, chansons, ballades

Examples:

a. Adam de la Hale (c. 1237–1288), *Le Jeu de Robin et de Marion*

b. *Song of Roland*

- 11th century—polyphony replaced monophony.

- 12th century—Notre Dame organum (Paris)

    Composers:

    a. Léonin

    b. Pérotin

- (c. 1240) *Sumer is icumen in*—oldest surviving piece of secular polyphony.

- Motet—began as sacred form and became secularized.

    Composer: Philippe de Vitry, (1291–1361)

- *Roman de Fauvel:* 14th-century collection

- 14th-century mass settings

    Composers:

    a. Tournai

    b. Toulouse

    c. Barcelona

    d. Guillaume de Machaut (c. 1304–1377) leading 14th-century composer, best known for *Messe de Notre Dame*

- 14th-century Italian madrigal

    Composer: Landini (1325–1397) (ballata)

- England: *The Old Hall Manuscript Collection*

- John Dunstable—leading English composer:

    Examples:

    a. *Veni Creator Spiritus* (motet)

    b. *Quam Pulcra es*

## Renaissance

- Composers of chansons, ballades, virelais, motets, and masses:

    Examples:

    a. Guillaume Dufay (c. 1400–1474) *Se la face ay pale* (mass)

    b. Binchois (c. 1400–1460)

    c. Johannes de Ockeghem, (c. 1420–1497) *Missa prolationum*

    d. Heinrich Isaac (c. 1450–1517)

- Jacob Obrecht (1450–1505)

- Josquin des Prés (1460–1521) composed twenty masses, seventy-five secular pieces, one hundred motets

- *Harmonice Musices Odhecaton A*—anthology

- *The Fitzwilliam Virginal Book* (English collection)—contains works by Bull, Byrd, Gibbons, Tomkins, Farnaby, and other contemporaries.

- Madrigalists: Gibbons, Orlando di Lasso, Victoria, Byrd

- Gesualdo (1560–1613) *Moro lasso al mio duolo*

- John Dowland (1563–1626) *The King of Denmark's Galliard*

- Martin Luther: The chorale setting (Reformation)

- Palestrina (1525–1594) (Counter-Reformation)

    Example: *Missa Papae Marcelli*

- Claudio Monteverdi (1567–1643)

    Examples:

    a. *Orfeo*
       *Poppea*

- Giovanni Gabrieli (1557–1612)

  Examples:

  a. *Sonata pian' e forte*
  b. *In ecclesiis*
  c. *Sacrae Symphoniae*

## Other Renaissance Composers

- Cipriano de Rore (1516–1565)

- Clemens (c. 1510–1556)

- Gombert (c. 1500–1556)

- Janequin (c. 1485–1560)

- Thomas Tallis (c. 1505–1585)

# Baroque

- Michael Praetorius (1571–1621)

  Example: *Musae Sioniae*

- Heinrich Schütz (1585–1672)

  Examples:

  a. *The Seven Last Words*
  b. *Symphoniae Sacrae*
  c. *Psalmen Davids*
  d. *Christmas Oratorio*

- Samuel Scheidt (1587–1654)

  Example: *Banchetto Musicale*

- Johann Schein (1586–1630)

  Example: *Sacred Concertos*

- Jan Sweelink (1562–1621)
  Example: *Fantasia Chromatica*

- Girolamo Frescobaldi (1583–1643)
  Examples:
  a. *Toccata for the Elevation*
  b. *Fiori musicali*

- François Couperin (1668–1733)
  Example: *Parnassus*

- Arcangelo Corelli (1653–1713)
  Examples:
  a. *Op. 1 Sonata da chiesa*
  b. *Op. 4 Sonate da camera*
  c. *Op. 5 Solo Sonatas*

- Jean Baptiste Lully (1632–1687)
  Examples:
  a. *Alceste*
  b. *Le Bourgeois Gentilhomme*

- Jean Philippe Rameau (1683–1764)
  Example: *Castor et Pollux*

- Dietrich Buxtehude (1637–1707)
  Example: *Prelude and Fugue in E minor*

- Henry Purcell (1659–1695)
  Example: *Dido and Aeneas*

- Antonio Vivaldi (1678–1741)
  Examples:
  a. *The Seasons*
  b. *Ode for St. Cecilia's Day*
  c. *Concerto Grossos Op. 3*
  d. *Gloria*

- Johann Sebastian Bach (1685–1750)

  Examples:

  a. *St. Matthew Passion*

  b. *The Magnificat*

  c. *Brandenburg Concertos*

  d. *Well-Tempered Clavier*

  e. *Passacaglia in C minor for organ*

  f. *Toccata and Fugue in D minor for organ*

  g. *Partita in D minor for violin*

  h. *Trio Sonatas BWV 252–530*

  i. *Chromatic Fantasia and Fugue in D minor*

  j. *Six French Suites*

  k. *Coffee Cantata BMV 211*

  l. Cantatas

     #4 *Christ lag in Todesbanden*

     #92 *Ich hab' in Gottes Herz und Sinn*

  m. *Mass in B minor*

- George Philipp Telemann (1681–1767)

  Example: *Suite in A minor*

- George Frederic Handel (1685–1759)

  Examples:

  a. *The Harmonious Blacksmith*

  b. *Fireworks Music*

  c. *Water Music*

  d. *Rinaldo*

  e. *Orlando*

  f. *Judas Maccabaeus*

  g. *Op. 6 Concerto Grosso*

  h. *Messiah*

- Giovanni Battista Pergolesi (1710–1736)

  Examples:

  a. *La Serva Padrona*

  b. *Stabat Mater*

- Pachelbel (1653–1706)

# Classical

- Domenico Scarlatti (1685–1757)

  Example: *Essercizi for harpsichord*

- C. P. E Bach (1714–1788)

  Example: *Prussian Sonatas*

- Johann Stamitz (1717–1757)

  Examples:

  a. *Symphony in D major*

  b. *La Melodica Germanica*

- Christoph Willibald Gluck (1714–1787)

  Examples:

  a. *Orfeo ed Euridice*

  b. *Alceste*

- Muzio Clementi (1752–1832)

  Example: *Keyboard Sonatinas*

- Franz Joseph Haydn (1732–1809)

  Examples:

  a. *Symphonies 6, 7, 8*

  b. *Farewell Symphony 45*

  c. *Symphonies 85, 88*

  d. *Oxford Symphony 92*

  e. *Surprise Symphony 94*

  f. *Military Symphony 100*

    g. *The Creation*

    h. *Trumpet Concerto*

    i. *String Quartet Op. 76*

    j. *Piano Sonata in C No. 35*

- Wolfgang Amadeus Mozart (1756–1791)

    General Works:

    a. *Piano and Violin Sonata* K. 304

    b. *G Major Piano Trio*

    c. *Clarinet Quintet* K. 581

    d. Piano Sonatas, K. 496, K. 310

    e. *Haydn Quartets* K. 387, 421, 428, 458, 464, 465

    f. *Eine kleine Nachtmusik* K. 525

    g. *Requiem*

    h. *Concerto in $E^b$* for two pianos and orchestra K. 365

    i. *Piano Concerto in D minor* K. 466

    j. *Violin Concerto in A Major* K. 219

    Symphonies:

    a. *Haffner* K. 385

    b. *Prague* K. 504

    c. *Jupiter* K. 551

    d. *G Minor* K. 550

    e. *Linz* K. 444

    Operas:

    a. *The Magic Flute*

    b. *Don Giovanni*

    c. *The Marriage of Figaro*

## Transition: Classical/Romantic

- Ludwig Van Beethoven (1770–1827)

Examples:

a. Symphonies 1–9 (3, 5, 7,9)

b. *Missa Solemnis*

c. *Fidelio*

d. Piano Sonatas:

   *Pathétique*

   *Moonlight Sonata*

   *Waldstein*

   *Appassionata*

   *Diabelli Variations*

e. String quartets—Op. 18, Op. 59, Op. 95, Op. 133

f. *Piano Trio Op. 97 in B$^b$*

g. *Piano Concerto No. 5*

## Other Classical Composers

- G. B. Sammartini (1701–1775)

- Johann Christian Bach (1735–1782)

- A. Soler (1729–1783)

- Carl Ditters von Dittersdorf (1739–1799)

- Boccherini (1743–1805)

- Dussek (1760–1812)

## Romantic

- Franz Peter Schubert (1797–1828)

Examples:

a. *Lieder* (songs):

   *Gretchen am Spinnrad*

   *Erlkönig*

   *Der Doppelgänger*

    b. *Moments Musicaux* D. 789

    c. *Drei Klavierstücke* D. 946

    d. *Forellen (Trout) Quintet*

    e. *Quartet in A minor* D. 804

    f. *Unfinished Symphony*

    g. *C major Symphony*

    h. *Mass in $E^b$* D. 950

- Robert Schumann (1810–1856)

  Examples:

      a. *Lieder—Mondnacht*

      b. *Die beiden Grenadiere*

      c. *Symphonic Etudes*

      d. *Kreisleriana Op. 16*

      e. *Papillons*

      f. *Carnaval*

      g. *Scenes from Childhood Op. 15*

      h. *Piano Quintet Op. 44*

- Offenbach (1819–1880)

  Example: *Orpheus in Hades*

- Johannes Brahms (1833–1897)

  Examples:

      a. *Ballades Op. 10*

      b. Symphonies 1–4

      c. *Academic Festival Overture*

      d. *Leider—Sapphische Ode*

      e. *Piano Quartet in G minor Op. 25*

      f. *Piano Quintet in F minor Op. 34A*

      g. *Horn Trio Op. 40*

      h. *Clarinet Quintet in B minor Op. 115*

      i. *German Requiem*

      j. *Piano Concerto in B$^b$*

- Hector Berlioz (1803–1869)

  Examples:

  a. *Damnation of Faust*

  b. *Requiem*

  c. *Te Deum*

  d. *L'Enfance du Christ*

  e. *Symphonie Fantastique*

- Giuseppe Verdi (1813–1901)

  Examples:

  a. *Requiem*

  b. *Aida*

  c. *Falstaff*

  d. *La Traviata*

- Anton Bruckner (1824–1896)

  Examples:

  a. *Mass in E minor*

  b. *Symphony #7*

- Georges Bizet (1838–1875)

  Example: *Carmen*

- G. Rossini (1792–1868)

  Examples:

  a. *Otello*

  b. *The Barber of Seville*

- Charles Gounod (1818–1893)

  Examples:

  a. *St. Cecilia*

  b. *Faust*

- Felix Mendelssohn-Bartholdy (1809–1847)

    Examples:

    a. *The Hebrides (Fingal's Cave)*

    b. *Midsummer Night's Dream*

    c. *Elijah*

    d. *Songs without Words*

    e. *Piano Trio in D minor Op. 49*

    f. *Italian Symphony*

    g. *Violin Concerto in E minor*

- Frederic Chopin (1810–1849)

    Examples:

    a. *Fantasia in F minor Op. 49*

    b. *Sonata in B$^b$*

    c. *B$^b$ minor Scherzo*

    d. *Fantaisie Impromptu*

    e. *A$^b$ major Polonaise*

    f. *A minor Prelude*

- Franz Liszt (1811–1886)

    Examples:

    a. *Etudes de Concert for piano*

    b. *Faust Symphony*

    c. *Piano Concerto in Eb*

    d. *Mephisto Waltz*

    e. *Les Prelúdes*

- Modest Mussorgsky (1839–1881)

    Examples:

    a. *Pictures at an Exhibition*

    b. *Boris Godunov*

- César Franck (1822–1890)

    Example: *Symphony in D minor*

- Antonin Dvorák (1841–1904)

    Examples:

    a. *New World Symphony*

    b. *American String Quartet*

- Hugo Wolf (1860–1909)

    Composed 250 *lieder*

- Peter Ilyich Tchaikovsky (1840–1893)

    Examples:

    a. *Swan Lake*

    b. *Sleeping Beauty*

    c. *The Nutcracker Suite*

    d. *1812 Overture*

- Richard Wagner (1813–1883)

    Examples:

    a. *Flying Dutchman*

    b. *Tannhäuser*

    c. *Lohengrin*

    d. *The Ring*

    e. *Tristan und Isolde*

    f. *Die Meistersinger*

- Gustav Mahler (1860–1911)

    Examples:

    a. *The Song of the Earth*

    b. *9th Symphony*

- Richard Strauss (1864–1949)

    Examples:

    a. *Traum durch die Dämmerung*

    b. *Tod und Verklärung*

    c. *Also sprach Zarathustra*

    d. *Till Eulenspiegels*

    e. *Salome*

    f. *Elektra*

- Camille Saint-Saëns (1835–1921)

  Examples:

      a. *G minor Piano Concerto*

      b. *Le Carnival des Animaux*

- Rimsky-Korsakov (1844–1908)

  Examples:

      a. *Capriccio espagnol*

      b. *Scheherazade*

- Alexander Scriabin (1872–1915)

  Example: *Prometheus*

- Edvard Grieg (1843–1907)

  Examples:

      a. *Piano Concerto in A minor*

      b. *Peer Gynt*

- Jean Sibelius (1865–1957)

  Example: *Finlandia*

- Giacomo Puccini (1858–1924)

  Examples:

      a. *La Bohème*

      b. *Tosca*

      c. *Madame Butterfly*

## Other Romantic Composers

- Borodin (1833–1887)

- Elgar (1857–1934)

- Glinka (1804–1857)
- Hummel (1778–1837)
- Pierné (1863–1937)
- Smetana (1824–1884)
- Spohr (1784–1859)

## Other Late Romantic/Early Twentieth-Century Composers

- Granados (1867–1916)
- Albéniz (1860–1909)
- MacDowell (1861–1908)
- Reger (1873–1916)
- Respighi (1879–1936)

## French Music—Post-Romantic

- Vincent d'Indy (1851–1931)
  Example: *Istar*
- Gabriel Fauré (1845–1924)
  Examples:
  a. *Clair de Lune*
  b. Impromptus, preludes, barcarolles, nocturnes for piano
  c. *Requiem*
- Claude Debussy (1862–1918)
  Examples:
  a. For piano:
  *Estampes*
  *Images*
  *Preludes*
  *Suite Bergamasque*

    *Pour le Piano*

    *Children's Corner*

  b. *String Quartet in G minor*

  c. *La Mer*

  d. *Prélude à l'après-midi d'un faune*

  e. *Danses*

  f. *Pelléas et Mélisande*

- Erik Satie (1866–1925)

  Example: *Gymnopédies for piano*

- Maurice Ravel (1875–1937)

  Examples:

  a. *String Quartet*

  b. Piano:

      *Jeux d'eau*

      *Le Tombeau de Couperin*

      *Gaspard de la nuit*

      *Valses nobles et sentimentales*

      *Mother Goose Suite*

  c. *Rapsodie Espagnole*

  d. *Bolero*

  e. *Pavane for a Deceased Infant*

  f. *Daphnis et Choloé*

  g. *Introduction and Allegro*

- Paul Dukas (1865–1935)

  Example: *The Sorcerer's Apprentice*

- Sergei Rachmaninoff (1873–1943)

  Example: *2nd Piano Concerto*

## Twentieth Century

- Béla Bartók (1881–1945)

Examples:

a. *Mikrokosmos*

b. *Allegro Barbaro*

c. *Duke Bluebeard's Castle*

d. *Cantata Profana*

e. *Concerto for Orchestra*

f. *Music for Strings, Percussion, and Celesta*

g. *Six String Quartets*

- Sergei Prokofiev (1891–1953)

  Examples:

  a. *3rd Piano Concerto*

  b. *Peter and the Wolf*

  c. *Romeo and Juliet*

  d. *The Love of Three Oranges*

- Ernest Bloch (1880–1959)

  Example: *String Quartet*

- Ralph Vaughn Williams (1872–1958)

  Examples:

  a. *Fantasia on a Theme by Thomas Tallis*

  b. *London Symphony*

- Gustav Holst (1874–1934)

  Example: *The Planets*

- Benjamin Britten (1913–1976)

  Examples:

  a. *A Ceremony of Carols*

  b. *War Requiem*

- Roy Harris (1898–1979)

  Example: *3rd Symphony*

- George Gershwin (1898–1937)

  Examples:

  a. *Rhapsody in Blue*

  b. *Porgy and Bess*

  c. *An American in Paris*

- Aaron Copland (1900– )

  Examples:

  a. *El Salón Mexico*

  b. *Billy the Kid*

  c. *Appalachian Spring*

  d. *Fanfare for the Common Man*

- Arthur Honegger (1892–1955)

  Example: *King David*

- Darius Milhaud (1892–1974)

  Examples:

  a. *The Creation of the World*

  b. *Suite Provencal*

- Francis Poulenc (1899–1963)

  Example: *Mass in G*

- Paul Hindemith (1895–1963)

  Examples:

  a. *Mathis der Maler*

  b. *Ludus Tonalis*

- Olivier Messiaen (1908– )

  Examples:

  a. *Oiseaux exotique*

  b. *Chronochromie*

  c. *Quartet for the End of Time*

- Charles Ives (1874–1954)

    Example: *Concord Sonata*

- Igor Stravinsky (1882–1971)

    Examples:

    a. *Fire Bird*

    b. *Petrushka*

    c. *Rite of Spring*

    d. *L'Historie du Soldat*

    e. *Octet for Wind Instruments*

    f. *The Rake's Progress*

    g. *Oedipus Rex*

    h. *Symphony of Psalms*

- Samuel Barber (1910–1981)

    Example: *Adagio for Strings*

- Arnold Schoenberg (1874–1951)

    Examples:

    a. *Pierrot Lunaire*

    b. *Variations for Orchestra*

    c. *Ode to Napoleon*

    d. *Verklärte Nacht*

- Alban Berg (1885–1935)

    Examples:

    a. *Lyric Suite*

    b. *Wozzeck*

- Anton Webern (1883–1945)

    Example: *Symphony Op. 21*

- Stockhausen (1928– )

    Examples:

    a. *Hymnen*

    b. *Song of the Young Man*

- Edgar Varèse (1883–1965)
  Example: *Ionisation*

- Milton Babbitt (1916– )
  Example: *Philomel*

- Pierre Boulez (1925– )
  Example: *Le Marteau Sans Maître*

## Other Twentieth-Century Composers

- Kodály (1882–1967)

- Kabalevsky (1904– )

- Piston (1894–1976)

- Shostakovich (1906–1975)

- Ginastera (1916–1983)

- Villa-Lobos (1887–1959)

- Carter (1908– )

- Ibert (1890–1962)

- Sessions (1896–1985)

- Howard Hanson (1896–1981)

- Cowell (1897–1965)

- Cage (1912– )

# *INTERLUDE*

---

It is good to give thanks to Yahweh,
to play in honor of your name, Most High,
to proclaim your love at daybreak
and your faithfulness all through the night
to the music of the zither and lyre,
to the rippling of the harp.

I am happy, Yahweh, at what you have done;
at your achievements I joyfully exclaim,
"Great are your achievements, Yahweh."

(Psalms 92:1–5a, TJB)

But let all who take refuge in you be glad;
    let them ever sing for joy.
Spread your protection over them,
    that those who love your name may rejoice in you.

(Psalms 5:11)

# 5

## DEVELOPING A WELL-ROUNDED MUSICIAN

*God rises to shouts of acclamation,*
*Yahweh rises to a blast of trumpets,*
*let the music sound for our God,*
*let it sound,*
*let the music sound for our King,*
*let it sound!*
*God is King of the whole world:*
*play your best in his honor!*

Psalms 47.5–7, TJB

Developing fine musicianship is the goal of all music education methods. Fine musicianship refers to having a comprehensive, thorough, well-rounded background in music. Like other education fields, good music education is approached systematically with clearly defined goals.

Music making is complex. The music educator's job is to guide students through mastering its many skills. This goal stands in stark contrast to a too commonly found phenomenon exemplified here: Linda has studied the violin for ten years. She can read music and play many pieces on the violin, *but* she has only a basic music theory background and has no knowledge of music history beyond her instrument. She has not been exposed to any other instruments, cannot transpose music, has not sung in a choir or played in an orchestra, cannot readily sightread or sightsing, and cannot improvise or compose. Linda is not a well-rounded musician, and her severe limitations could have been avoided.

## The Parent's Role

Now we come to the reason that this book is written primarily for parents. No single music educator can meet all these needs at your child's different age levels. The finest music educators leading school, community, or church music programs encourage students to study privately to excel on their individual instruments. The finest private music teachers encourage their students to become involved in group music experiences. Ultimately, parents need to oversee the direction of their children's musical progress with vision, dedication, plain hard work, and research.

My own parents were not musicians, nor were they wealthy, but they were dedicated to providing me with an arts education. Singing, listening to records, and dance lessons were part of my early childhood. Dalcroze, Kodály, Orff-Schulwerk, and Suzuki were unheard of then! I began studying the piano privately at age six. During my elementary school years I studied with a teacher whose greatest strength was teaching sight reading. In junior high school my next teacher introduced me to serious literature, but her greatest strength was teaching jazz improvisational piano. In senior high school my teacher, who trained at Julliard, focused on serious literature, musical nuances, performance, theory, and history to prepare me for college. Along the way I had the opportunity to study other instruments and play in an orchestra. Throughout high school I accompanied choral groups and instrumentalists and sang in choirs. Each of my music teachers gave me an invaluable skill, but I am most grateful to my parents, who supervised the whole picture and wove the opportunities together.

As you plan your child's music training, set up preliminary interviews with music teachers to discuss their offerings. Find out what their backgrounds are, their specializations, the methods they employ, their professional affiliations, and where they are performing—so that you can hear them play. Visit their programs and listen to their students. Building a solid foundation for students is the most important step. Sometimes parents assume that beginning students can start out with "beginning teachers." The opposite is true. Beginners need the *best* teachers to start out right.

## Musicianship Guidelines

You are looking for an excellent musician and for a music educator who teaches all aspects of music beyond a specific instrument. Whether you are researching school or church music programs or private music teachers, look for the qualities listed below.

1. Above all else, the student should learn to make *beautiful music*. Playing the written notes is not enough; the music must "work." We know it when we hear it. The music dances; the phrases are shaped; there is dynamic contrast. We know that the musician feels what he or she is playing. The pianist who plays the notes without musical feeling might as well be typing! The music educator must be a fine musician in order to teach this most important skill. It can only be learned with the help of a good model. The old saying "Those who can't do, teach" is laughable here. Music instructors can only teach literature that they can play beautifully.

2. The student should enjoy integrated music experiences in Dalcroze, Kodály, Orff-Schulwerk, and Suzuki beginning in early childhood and continuing through adolescence.

3. The student should be exposed to a variety of music styles including folk literature, serious art music, rock, and jazz.

   A well-rounded musician can perform a Bach suite as well as improvise or play in a pit orchestra. A well-rounded musician should never have to say, "I don't play that style."

4. The student should understand the history of music and play and listen to works from each period. In my own group classes, the listening assignment is a composer per month.

5. When ready, students should be encouraged to choose an individual instrument to excel on through private study. Ideally, the private teacher has a group class program to augment private lessons. It is simply impossible for a private teacher to cover all facets of music in one lesson per week focused on a single instrument. Technical mastery of the instrument is a prerequisite to being able to make beautiful music. The ability to teach correct technique is another important factor in choosing a private teacher.

6. Students should learn music theory to be able to analyze harmony and form in music, transpose, improvise, and enjoy composing and orchestrating their own creations. The "tools of the trade" should be theirs. Ear training should include dictation (writing down what they hear).

7. Students should learn to read music fluently. Numerous method series exist for each instrument.

   Students should learn to sight-sing, hear the music internally, and sight-read on their instrument. We should note here that the only way to learn these skills is to *practice doing* them. There is no magic "gift."

8. Students should be encouraged to have choral and orchestral ensemble experiences. Learning choral and orchestral parts is as important as learning solo literature. All musicians should sing in a choir at some point. Orchestral playing is just as valuable but is not as financially or logistically accessible. If local schools do not offer choir or orchestra, investigate city youth symphonies, choirs, or summer music camps.

9. Students should have regular opportunities to share ("perform") their pieces with others in a safe, cooperative atmosphere free from pressure or competition. This is the greatest advantage of group classes (versus recitals).

10. It is critical that older students know their skills are useful, relevant, and do socially involve them with their peers. Vocalists in choirs, instrumentalists in orchestras, pianists with accompanying jobs are all examples of application. Without a way to apply their skills, teenage musicians often lose interest and drop out of music lessons.

11. Students should be exposed to other instruments beyond their own. Some knowledge of the keyboard is indispensable to brass, string, and wind players as well as vocalists, equipping them to think "orchestrally" (chordally) versus the one line melody often played on their instruments. This is essential to learning music theory. Pianists can only benefit from trying to play an instrument that they must work to "play in tune." Every musician should have basic exposure to the four instrument families.

In my own group classes we have a lecture-demonstration with hands-on exploration to introduce the different instrument families. All students learn to play the recorder (the most basic wind instrument), assorted Orff-Schulwerk instruments, and are introduced to guitar. All my students meet my goal of basic exposure to the different instruments, and sometimes a student will take a liking to one and begin to study that instrument privately.

Each year my students orchestrate either a piano piece or an original composition. The "ensemble" is performed for our group class complete with a variety of instruments and a conductor. The older students actually write their piece out in score.

When investigating the world of music with your child, you will find the instruments are categorized into families (see table 2 and also appendix A for further information on individual instruments.)

| Table 2: Orchestral Instruments | |
|---|---|
| **Strings** | **Woodwinds** |
| Violin<br>Viola<br>Violoncello<br>Double Bass | Piccolo<br>Flute<br>Oboe<br>English Horn<br>Clarinet<br>Bass Clarinet<br>Bassoon<br>Contra Bassoon |
| **Brass** | **Percussion** |
| Trumpet<br>French Horn<br>Trombone (Tenor, Bass)<br>Tuba | Chimes<br>Cymbals, Gong, Triangle<br>Drums: Snare, Tenor, Bass<br>Glockenspiel<br>Marimba<br>Timpani (Kettledrums)<br>Vibraphone<br>Xylophone |
| **Special Categories** | |
| Celesta<br>Cornet<br>Guitar<br>Harp<br>Piano, Organ, Harpsichord<br>Saxophone | |
| **Folk Instruments** | |
| Banjo<br>Folk Harp (Troubadour)<br>Recorder (Soprano, Alto, Tenor)<br>Zither | Dulcimer<br>Mandolin<br>Ukulele |

## Recommended for Listening
## (An Introduction to Orchestra)

- Britten, B. *A Young Person's Guide to the Orchestra.*

- Kleinsinger, G. and Tripp, P. *Tubby the Tuba.* (for the young child)

- Prokofiev, S. *Peter and the Wolf.*

## Voice

The approximate ranges for children's voices are:

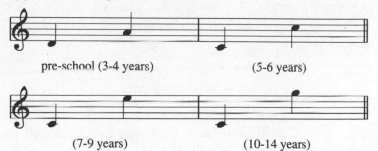

pre-school (3-4 years)          (5-6 years)

(7-9 years)                (10-14 years)

Not many people realize that the voice is a serious instrument. Correct use of the vocal cords is a complex task requiring years of training to master. Even as having a flute in your home and knowing how to play *Twinkle, Twinkle, Little Star* do not make you a flautist, having a nice voice and singing folk tunes do not make you a singer.

Serious vocalists are well-trained musicians. Experts agree that young people should not receive serious vocal training, which includes stretching the voice range and singing adult literature, until they complete their physical growth, generally over sixteen years old, when height is reached. The vocal cords are growing muscles. Training a voice before it is physically ready can actually cause damage. Children should be encouraged to sing naturally in their range, be involved in choir, and be taught to sing correctly. But they should not be singing adult repertoire requiring adult ranges.

Many young people damage their voices by trying to emulate that forced sound of rock singers. That sound is the rubbing together of the vocal cords, which creates callouses, ruining the voice. Eventually these recording stars, unable to sing anymore, suffer the short-lived career typical of that industry. Constant yelling, such as cheerleading, has the same effect.

When choosing a voice teacher, use the same criteria as choosing an instrumental teacher. The teacher should be well-trained, have a solid background in voice literature, and use correct technique on his or her instrument.

Because it is an instrument, *everyone* can improve his or her voice with training. A nice voice is a gift. The task to develop it fully, as for any instrument, requires dedicated practice and plain hard work.

## Developing Pianists

We devote a separate section to the piano because it is the most commonly studied instrument. Piano and organ are also the instruments most often played in church settings.

Keyboard skills are invaluable to any musician. Universities require all music majors to reach a certain level of proficiency on the piano. But it is one thing to learn keyboard as a secondary instrument and quite another to become a fluent pianist, which requires a thorough instructional program.

A fluent pianist is a functional pianist. The term *functional* is defined as useful, developed to serve a function. All musicians need to be functional and have skills beyond performing their solo literature. Vocalists learn to read choral scores in choir. Orchestral musicians become familiar with orchestral literature for group performance. But often fine solo pianists do not become functional pianists.

As a young person in high school I attended a dinner party honoring a young concert pianist. She was my age and was concertizing in the area. After dinner we were privileged to hear this young artist play one of her most impressive pieces. I marveled at her musicianship, her poise, and her love for performing. Though I had studied the piano for years and was playing literature similar to hers in local recitals, I had no love affair with solo performing! Then an interesting thing happened.

The dinner guests began to gather around the piano and wanted to sing. They assumed that this young artist could play for them and began putting books of music up on the piano. But her expression turned from triumph to terror, and my heart went out to her. She tried to play for them, but she could not. She couldn't sight-read. She couldn't transpose or improvise. She had never seen a lead sheet or a score. She couldn't accompany the vocalist who had been asked to sing. She wasn't *functional.*

Having marveled at her talents, I was shocked. I was not a concert performer, but I had worked as an accompanist since I was twelve. I couldn't understand how this young artist could be so outstanding at one level of musicianship and so inadequate at another. A few of the guests knew that I was also a pianist and asked if I could accompany the vocalist. I agreed, and the guests sang as I played for them until midnight.

I thought that this incident was highly unusual until I reached college and then graduate school. I was surprised to find that most serious piano students up into the doctoral level were deficient in functional skills. When I became a piano educator, I dedicated my efforts to developing well-rounded pianists with the following skills:

*In addition to:*

- fine musicianship;

- a background in music history and music theory (knowledge of figured bass);

- experience playing works from the Renaissance, Baroque, Classical, Romantic and Twentieth-Century periods; and

- a mastery of technique,

*functional pianists:*

- can sightread fluently;

- can transpose music to other keys;

- can play in ensemble with other musicians:

  a. duets and duo-piano works—the first step in learning to accompany other instrumentalists,

  b. accompaniment for solo vocalists and instrumentalists and for choirs,

  c. chamber ensembles (chamber music) and orchestras;

- are comfortable with score reading:

  a. four-part choral score,

  b. alto and tenor clef in preparation for reading orchestral scores;

- are familiar with the role of the piano as "orchestra":

  a. playing orchestral reductions (i.e., accompanying choral oratorios or instrumental concertos),

  b. playing in a pit orchestra;

- are exposed to playing other keyboard instruments: organ, harpsichord, clavichord, synthesizer;

- know all chord types, can improvise and read a lead sheet, applying music theory to functional practice, which requires a knowledge of contemporary styles; and

- have explored arranging, composing, and orchestrating (giving different parts to the various instruments).

The only way to learn these listed skills is actually to experience them. You can't learn "about" accompanying. You must actually do it! First attempts will be very easy, and the effort will rapidly lead to extensive opportunities. A fluent pianist who is a good accompanist always has work. Those jobs were my "bread and butter" all through school. Pianists have the most difficult task because they must "learn it all."

In keeping with the understanding that music education has specific techniques for reaching set goals, Appendix L offers a detailed piano fluency program. While a detailed program for *every* instrument is beyond the scope of this book, the piano plan can serve as a model for outlining study programs for other instruments. Obviously literature and techniques will vary but the goals of fluency and comprehensive musicianship remain the same.

# *INTERLUDE*

---

But I will sing of your strength,
  in the morning I will sing of your love;
for you are my fortress,
  my refuge in times of trouble.

(Psalms 59:16)

Because you are my help,
  I sing in the shadow of your wings.

(Psalms 63:7)

My heart is ready, God
—I mean to sing and play.
  Awake, my muse,
awake, lyre and harp,
  I mean to wake the Dawn!

Yahweh, I mean to thank you among the peoples,
  to play music to you among the nations;
your love is high as heaven,
  your faithfulness as the clouds.
Rise high above the heavens, God,
  let your glory be over the earth!

To bring rescue to those you love
save with your right hand and answer us!

(Psalms 108:1–6, TJB)

# 6

## MUSIC THERAPY: MUSIC IS FOR ALL GOD'S PEOPLE

*When people groan
under the weight of oppression,
or cry out under the tyranny of the mighty,
no one thinks to ask,
"Where is God, my maker,
who makes glad songs ring out
at dead of night?"*

Job 35:9–10, TJB

We have already established that music education is not limited to the "talented," but can that be carried to the opposite extreme? Is music experience intended for the blind, crippled, deaf, developmentally- or learning-disabled, emotionally disturbed, aging, and dying? Is music education for the "imperfect"?

The Biblical answer is undeniably yes. God intended music to be a gift and tool for *all* His people, especially to comfort those who are hurting. Scripture commands us minister to the suffering with music:

75

> It is to treat a wound with vinegar
> to sing songs to a sorrowing heart. (Proverbs 25:20,
> TJB)

King Hezekiah lay dying when Isaiah, his pastoral counselor, encouraged the king to compose a canticle to express his sorrow and frustration (see Isaiah 38). Today creative arts therapies are accepted grief counseling techniques to encourage the expression of feelings.

David may have been the first music therapist. Note how David treated King Saul's mental anguish:

> Now the spirit of Yahweh had left Saul and an evil spirit from Yahweh filled him with terror. Saul's servants said to him, "Look, an evil spirit of God is the cause of your terror. Let our lord give the order, and your servants who wait on you will look for a skilled harpist; when the evil spirit of God troubles you, the harpist will play and you will recover." Saul said to his servants, "Find me a man who plays well and bring him to me." And whenever the spirit from God troubled Saul, David took the harp and played; then Saul grew calm, and recovered, and the evil spirit left him. (1 Samuel 16:14–17, 23, TJB)

Music therapy is a professional specialization but has applications for all of us. Having worked as a church musician for fifteen years, I fully support that ministry, but I believe that church service music (choir anthems, musicals, congregational singing, and the like), no matter how wonderful, is the *beginning* of music ministry, not the accomplished end. I contend that music therapy is perhaps the secular, professional term for the *ministry* of music, as a branch of pastoral care.

## Music Therapy Defined

Music therapy can be defined as the treatment of disorders and problems through music. It is one of the creative art therapies, which also include art, dance, and drama therapy. Creative arts therapists employ their artistic mediums to influence behavior change. Music making is an effective tool because it is one of the few processes that involves all our modalities—visual, auditory, motor, emotional, cognitive, and so on. It is cross-modal. While we comfortably employ a strong developmental area, we can simultaneously work on a weak developmental area. Music making provides a secure, nonthreatening environment in which a trusting relationship with the therapist can be easily established. The client is distracted from his limitations, and the disorder is more easily treated. Thus music therapy techniques can benefit counseling sessions. Music therapists incorporate art, movement, and creative dramatics techniques when appropriate.

In schools and hospitals or in private practice, music therapists work with a variety of exceptional children, the chronically and terminally ill, the aging, the mentally ill, individuals in crisis, and any population with special needs.

Music therapy in the clinical setting can help an accident victim to regain the use of his hands as he learns to play an instrument. It can be used to teach a developmentally disabled child how to socialize with others through musical games or can help a newborn infant to discover his environment. It can relieve stress through imagery and relaxation techniques. Music therapy is the use of familiar songs to prompt an aging, terminally ill patient to discuss life experiences and prepare for death. It provides music in the delivery room to ease the birth process. Music therapy can teach individuals with respiratory disorders or speech problems to sing. It is implementing group music activities to enhance the self-esteem of psychiatric patients. Music therapy employs musical games and songs to encourage a child abuse victim to discuss the experience or to distract a pediatric patient from pain and alleviate the trauma of hospitalization.

Music therapy in the church is using Orff-Schulwerk activities to prompt children to discuss their relationships with God or teaching Braille music to enable the visually impaired to use a

Braille hymnal. The applications are endless. Once the need is identified, the musical experience can be tailored to meet it.

Working as a church musician and a music therapist in a children's hospital with chronically and terminally ill children, I found my jobs to be much alike though I was paid by different sources. In visitation at home or at a hospital bedside, I implemented music therapy sessions with the sick and dying to distract them from pain and alleviate the stress of illness and hospitalization. Knowing that verbalization precedes understanding and mastery of anxiety, I integrated musical activities with an understanding of God's presence and comfort to prompt discussion of the patient's fears and anxieties about illness and death.

In the church, I have led a children's choir in music therapy sessions on Sunday mornings. Each week a different theme was presented in musical games structured to enable each child to verbalize his or her relationship with God and express feelings through playing Orff instruments. Some of the themes were prayer (made analogous to "talking to one's best friend"), praise and thanksgiving, and caring for others. The goal was each child's developed relationship with God. You will find a collection of pastoral care/music therapy songs that I have used in Appendix K.

## The Training of Music Therapists

Music therapists are trained at universities that offer a music therapy program approved by the National Association for Music Therapy. They earn a bachelor's degree with a major in music combined with studies in psychology, special education, sociology, anatomy, related creative arts, and other fields related to therapy. Each semester, field work with a different disability is required. After degree completion music therapists intern for six months at an approved facility to become registered and take an exam to be board certified. Many specialize at the graduate level.

# Music for All Abilities:
# Educating the Exceptional

Music education for the exceptional is a natural extension of music therapy. With the passing of Public Law 94–142 in the 1970s, every exceptional child gained the legal right to music education. Music educators looked to their colleagues in music therapy for a foundation in working with disability. Public and private music educators as well as music therapists began to understand that Kodály, Dalcroze, Orff-Schulwerk, and Suzuki provided the needed link. Therapeutic and arts educational goals could be met simultaneously through these approaches.

The basic principles of the methods do not change when applied to the exceptional. Teachers adapt by moving at a slower pace, requiring more repetition, and breaking down tasks into the smallest parts possible.

Once the focus of music education became developmental music experiences (as opposed to music reading), effective music education could be provided for all types of exceptional children. A severely developmentally disabled child who may never read music can still receive music *education*.

Learning to make music on an instrument is one of the most complex tasks a human being can approach. It involves all perceptual, cognitive, and kinesthetic processes simultaneously and is the highest integration of developmental skills. Learning to play an instrument can be a therapeutic process and, for the motivation of the student, there is a quality product. The development of the whole person remains the goal.

Of course, the exceptional are not denied music reading skills. These skills are simply taught according to ability. The blind, for example, can be taught Braille music.

# Music Education for All Ages

When we think of music education, most of us think "children." At one time we associated music education only with school-age children. Today we have expanded that view to include infants, toddlers, and preschoolers.

Now we need to extend the other way! Education is not limited by a person's age. We are never too young or too old to learn a new skill. Remember that the Suzuki method educates parents as well as children. Music education is intended for adults and the aging as well. Dalcroze, Kodály, Orff-Schulwerk, Suzuki, and the other techniques of developing comprehensive musicianship have been successfully applied with older age groups, too.

Just as musically educating exceptional children requires a knowledge of different disabilities, musically educating the aging requires a knowledge of gerontology. Music therapists/educators integrate effective music education methods with a knowledge of special populations.

## Music and Imagery

The role of music and imagery needs to be discussed before leaving this topic. We Christians are concerned about imagery today for good reason. We fear its use with New Age practices and meditation techniques. We are quick to associate it with evil. But we need to be discerning.

Imagery comes from the word "imagine." Our imagination is a creative gift from God. Imagery means to form a mental picture. The book of Psalms is full of imagery. The use of Scripture, prayer, and music are pure forms of imagery.

Health care professionals, including hospital chaplains, use music imagery with patients for relaxation and pain reduction. Imagery is used therapeutically in counseling sessions. Even music education students enjoy imagining stories inspired by the pieces they are playing.

Imagery in itself is not evil, but its purposes can be godly or ungodly. We must ask if the mental pictures formed are pure and Biblically based. Imagine reading the Psalms while playing hymn music for a dying patient, helping them to feel protected by God. The key is that the mental pictures help us focus on God, not draw us away from God.

The *ministry* of music is intended for *all* God's people. As music educator, music therapist, or parent, we each have the privilege of sharing the gift of music with people of all ages and abilities.

# *INTERLUDE*

---

Sing Yahweh a new song
   for he has performed marvels,
his own right hand, his holy arm,
   gives him the power to save.

Yahweh has displayed his power;
has revealed his righteousness to the nations,
mindful of his love and faithfulness
   to the house of Israel.

The most distant parts of the earth have seen
   the saving power of our God.
Acclaim Yahweh, all the earth,
   burst into shouts of joy!

Sing to Yahweh, sing to the music of harps,
   and to the sound of many instruments;
to the sound of trumpet and horn
   acclaim Yahweh the King!

Let the sea thunder and all that it holds,
   and the world, with all who live in it;
let all the rivers clap their hands
   and the mountains shout for joy,

at the presence of Yahweh, for he comes
   to judge the earth,
to judge the world with righteousness
   and the nations with strict justice.

(Psalm 98, TJB)

# 7

## THE WELL-ROUNDED ARTIST: AN INTEGRATED ARTS APPROACH

*The heavens declare the glory of God,*
*the vault of heaven proclaims*
*his handiwork.*

Psalms 19:1, TJB

Our God, the Creator of the universe, is a master artist. His artistry is displayed in the colorful palette and sculpture of our world, in the drama and poetry of Scripture, in the theme of music making and dance that runs through His Word.

Throughout history, the great works of music, art, literature, and movement have been the attempts of human artists to capture and reflect God's original work.

Being a well-rounded artist is as important as being a well-rounded musician. The creative arts—art, dance, drama, music, and literature—are not separate categories. They are integrated pieces of the whole picture and should be studied as such. No one is expected to excel equally in all of these fields! Each requires years of serious study, and there are simply not enough hours in the day to pursue each field fully. But our children can be *exposed* to the related arts and will be better musicians for it. The same principles govern each artistic process and expand a view of our own craft. Each is a learned skill.

We learned in chapter 3 that movement/rhythm is the foundation of music ability. We have seen that creative music making methods include movement, literature, and creative dramatics.

## Creative Arts Activities

As a creative arts therapist, I enjoyed studying and integrating art and movement therapy and creative dramatics with my music therapy work. When I became a Suzuki music teacher, I discovered that it was just as important to integrate a full arts education approach with music education. The result was a summer creative arts program for my students.

Whether you locate a similar program or design your own, here are some guidelines to assist you:

1. The best time to implement an arts emphasis program is during summer and vacation breaks when a change from routine music lessons is desirable.

2. Professional art, dance, and drama teachers can be enlisted to teach or act as consultants on their areas of expertise.

3. The program should include arts *experience* as well as arts *appreciation/exposure*. Students should be painting, weaving, sculpting, moving, acting, making music, and writing; attending art museums, plays, the ballet, and the symphony; and reading great works of literature. Musicians especially enjoy poetry—music in words.

4. Separate art, dance, music, creative drama, and literature classes could be offered, or an integrated approach might work best. For example, the program could culminate in a performed "opera" with students' poems set to their

composed music, dancing, acting, sets painted, and other activities—all products of the children's experiences.

If such a performance is not feasible, it is still wise to integrate the arts experiences whenever possible. The students can paint their responses or dance to different great works of music, write lyrics to their musical compositions, act out scenes inspired by great paintings. The creative possibilities are endless. The goal of the creative arts program is full experience of the whole artistic process.

One of the best ways to integrate the arts for younger children is to read a story or poem and have the children:

- dramatize it, incorporating dance movements.

- create songs for it (music and lyrics).

- play instruments to realize the sounds in the story/poem.

- paint scenes from the story/poem.

- incorporate puppetry.

In addition to arts experience and appreciation, children should be learning the interconnected history of the arts. Music history is intimately tied to the history of arts, dance, and drama.

Becoming knowledgeable in the liberal arts is an important extension of studying the creative arts. Music is a complex subject that touches many fields. One cannot seriously study music without studying history, language, and literature as well. How can we study medieval music without understanding the history of the Middle Ages? How do we appreciate Hindemith's *Mathis der Mahler* based on the life and work of artist Matthias Grünewald? How can we fully experience Debussy's music if we have never seen a French impressionist painting or understand his music instructions without exposure to French? How do we grasp the genre of opera if we have no knowledge of the great works of literature that inspired them? How do we play the music of the great ballets if we have never seen that dance form?

Our goal is not expertise; it is understanding through exposure, with music as the link in the process. I mentioned that my students listen to the music of one composer per month as part of my group class program. In addition, one student presents an arts overview of that composer to the class. The overview includes a look at the art work, dance forms, literature, and culture of that time to provide a thorough historical perspective for appreciating the music.

The artistic realm of our world is a treasure chest to open and enjoy for a lifetime. Our vision is to communicate that joyful discovery to our children.

## Early Childhood Arts Education

Just as early childhood is established as the best and most natural time to introduce music experiences, the same holds true for the related arts.

Apply the same guidelines of good music education to explore the arts. Take your cue from the child's development, not traditional methods. For example, preschoolers should not be restricted at the bar concentrating on the five ballet positions any more than they should be reading notes from the staff. Young artists should be engaged in whole body movement and exploration, creating dances, enacting stories, and moving to a wide range of musical styles. Today trained dance educators offer excellent creative dance programs for young children. Like music educators, dance educators employ childhood chants/songs and images to teach different dance techniques.

Arts educators provide young children with a variety of arts materials to experiment with and enjoy creating. Projects are planned for exploration. Never is a structured "right or wrong" expectation applied. Art and originality go hand in hand.

The home environment remains the key. Art and dance/drama programs are excellent opportunities, but one or two class hours per week cannot compare with an everyday home setting. Provide an open space where your children can dance and play a variety of music styles. (Yes, move the furniture! My older daughter now does this herself.) Read stories that they can enact. Keep a set of rhythm/Orff instruments available for play. Have an "art center" in your home with a variety of supplies always available for ongoing projects. (Table 3 lists some dance genres and art mediums to consider.) Lavishly display their art work around the house. Always be reading a quality work of literature. Fun and effective videotaped foreign language programs are even available for preschoolers.*

| Table 3: Dance and Art to Consider | |
| --- | --- |
| **Dance Genres to Consider** | **Art Mediums to Consider** |
| Ballet<br>Creative<br>Folk/Cultural<br>Jazz<br>Modern<br>Tap | Ceramics<br>Design<br>Drawing<br>Glass<br>Graphics<br>Lettering<br>Painting: Oils, Watercolor, Acrylics<br>Pastels<br>Pen and Ink<br>Photography<br>Printmaking<br>Regional Folk Arts<br>Sculpture<br>Textiles/Weaving |

These are tools to create a total arts environment for your family. It is no secret that it will also create a mess! Rearranged furniture and paint, clay, and ink on tables and floors, will not qualify for a page in *Better Homes and Gardens,* but we must be willing to sacrifice a little present-day art and design if we want to foster the development of future-day artists.

---

* Example: Muzzy—The BBC Language Course for Children (French, German, Italian, Spanish). Early Advantage, 47 Richards Ave, Norwalk, CT 06857.

Just as young music makers later select one instrument to excel on privately, young dancers will develop to concentrate on one dance form (such as ballet), and young artists will become skilled in a specific medium. The key is to offer a wide range of early experiences as a foundation. Artists trained from a wide base of exposure often develop several areas of expertise: musicians who play several instruments; dancers who are as comfortable with jazz as they are with ballet; artists who can sculpt as well as paint; and so on. These artists were never limited to one genre, so they understand a variety of styles. They also enjoy a whole historical perspective of the arts.

You will find an arts history overview in Appendix I and creative arts resources in Appendix C.

Note how God's entire creation praises Him:

The birds of the air nest by the waters; they sing among the branches. (Psalms 104:12)

Sing for joy, O heavens, for the LORD has done this; shout aloud, O earth beneath. Burst into song, you mountains, you forests and all you trees, for the LORD has redeemed Jacob, he displays his glory in Israel. (Isaiah 44:23)

You will go out in joy and be led forth in peace; the mountains and hills will burst into song before you, and all the trees of the field will clap their hands. (Isaiah 55:12)

Then the trees of the forest will sing, they will sing for joy before the LORD, for he comes to judge the earth. (1 Chronicles 16:33)

# *INTERLUDE*

---

Alleluia!

Sing Yahweh a new song,
let the congregation of the faithful sing his praise!
Let Israel rejoice in his maker,
and Zion's children exult in their King;
let them dance in praise of his name,
playing to him on strings and drums!

(Psalms 149:1–3, TJB)

For the grave cannot praise you,
   death cannot sing your praise;
those who go down to the pit
   cannot hope for your faithfulness.

(Isaiah 38:18)

# 8

## REAL-LIFE MUSIC EDUCATION: PRACTICAL TIPS FOR PARENTS

*Your decrees are the theme of my song*
*wherever I lodge.*

Psalms 119:54

For seven chapters I have spoken to you as a music educator. Now I want to speak to you as a fellow parent. For all my training, I have normal, real-life children like yours who "don't feel like practicing today" and, on worse days, fall on the piano, crying, "This is too hard! Why are you so mean to me? I want to quit. . . . My life is terrible." One daughter is especially dramatic about her imprisonment. She would much rather listen to the latest Amy Grant tape than her Suzuki tape (I say she can do both). When I took her to a Dalcroze program taught by a leading teacher, she refused to participate because "none of her friends were there." She watched intently and we both learned much. But this is the same daughter who constantly plays tapes on the stereo as she dances about the room. This is the same daughter who loves to play for group piano class and proudly takes her violin to school to play on Share Day. This is the same child who beams as she fiddles with her dad in the church talent show and is thrilled to have the lead in the Christmas musical. She loves to make music. She does *not* like to work at it. That is human nature. But guess what? You can't have one without the other.

I am amazed at the number of people who equate hard work with being miserable. I have found that I reap the greatest rewards from what I work hardest at—jobs, schooling, marriage, learning a new skill. When we pay the price to invest ourselves in a task, the gain is that much more valuable and meaningful. Perhaps it is the flip side of "Easy come, easy go." When we work hard toward a goal, the rewards are lasting.

How do we balance this with parents' often-asked question, "Am I pushing my child too much?" First of all, a parent should never push a child, especially into such a joyous task as music making. Our role is to encourage lovingly, support consistently, and provide the needed tools. One of my Suzuki parents says it beautifully to her six-year-old son: "God has given you a wonderful gift. Together we have to unwrap it." Unwrapping the gift of music is a long process. The paper, ribbon, and tape get stuck, and sometimes we're tempted to throw the whole thing away. Yet if we can get through the unwrapping, we will have given our children a jeweled treasure of lifetime enjoyment.

I am also a realist. Music is not going to be the center of every child's life. Many other valid activities and interests compete. But music education, like math, reading, Bible study, and other basics, can be part of every child's life. Our job is to offer the opportunity. Not every child needs to have private music lessons. A church choir or school music program can offer excellent training

Helping children not to give up is different from pushing them. These are warning signs that I have observed in parents who push too hard:

1. The parent is chronically angry and frustrated with the child's progress. (This is different from a bad day. We all have those!)

2. The parent has a competitive spirit and sees music lessons as an extension of "Teaching Your Baby to Read" or sports lessons—all at the earliest age possible.

3. The parent is trying to fulfill his or her own dreams and self-worth through the children. This often occurs in nonmusical parents who want to relive that opportunity.

4. The parent is more concerned with the child being the "best" than with an enjoyment of music. He or she doesn't take cues from the child's individual needs or abilities.

## Teaching Discipline

Having established that there is no place for pushing children, how do we realistically encourage them when they want to give up? We teach them discipline. We model a disciplined lifestyle. We can show our children how to persevere in the face of a difficult task. We are not only sharing with them the gift of music. We are passing on a Biblical life tool.

School teachers observe that their top students are often serious musicians or trained athletes. Are they multitalented? No! Their achievements are not as much a matter of ability as they are a result of learning discipline. Knowing how to approach hard work successfully transfers to every other skill in life.

The reason I confidently tell you that you can expect disciplined music making from your children is that I have lived through it. I was once that child, crying at the piano. I wanted to quit when the music got hard. I wanted to play out in the street with the neighborhood kids instead of practicing. But the house rule was that I finished my practice and homework before playtime. I gave my mother many bad days.

But ten years later when many of those kids who had been playing in the street were on drugs and alcohol, I was playing in choirs and orchestras, involved with other young people who loved music, winning scholarships and awards, going off to a wonderful college, and basically having the time of my life. My parents had given me the gift of skill and discipline, making life rich and meaningful.

It is a fact that what we learn as young children becomes most natural to us. Learning a musical instrument or a foreign language later in life is difficult and will probably never become natural. Transferring to another instrument later is not difficult once skills on one instrument are established. If we wait until children are old enough to want to be disciplined to study music, it will be too late.

On your worst days when your children balk at practice, remember this: I have *never* met an accomplished musician, athlete, or other skilled adult who says, "I wish my parents hadn't made me learn this." I have met scores of adults who tell me, "I would love to know how to do that (i.e., play an instrument) today. I wish my parents hadn't let me give up. It's too late now."

Skills developed during childhood will become adult play. Learning to swim, paint, dance, ski, play an instrument, read, ice skate, and so on may be work for your child now but someday these skills will bring adult joy and relaxation. When we give our children these tools with loving support, never pressure or judgment, they will be less likely to become bored as young adults and turn to drugs, alcohol, and sex.


## Helping Children Practice

Nine guidelines follow for helping children persevere through practice:

1. Set a regular daily practice time. Practicing at the same time every day will become routine. Hoping to fit it in never works.

2. Always keep instruments in tune. Children's ears are learning correct pitch.

3. Children need time to be children and to play. Do not schedule them in so many concurrent activities, learning an overwhelming variety of skills, that there is no time for them to relax. Remember, one accomplished skill will transfer to other areas, but several mediocre skills will not. Children who practice when they are exhausted and cannot concentrate are not gaining anything.

4. *How* children practice is the key, not *how much* they practice. Practicing four hours a day can accomplish nothing if it is done incorrectly. One can simply be practicing mistakes. Forty-five minutes of focused, correct practice can make a superb musician. Correct practice includes:

   a. Working out difficult sections individually.

   b. Figuring out good fingerings.

   c. Analyzing music away from the instrument. This is the best way to memorize.

   d. Experimenting with interpretation (phrasing, dynamic contrast, and so on).

   Never practice a piece by starting at the beginning every time; play till it breaks down, and then keep repeating it from the there. It is far more effective to focus on the trouble areas.

5. Respect your child's age and attention span. Preschoolers practice in short blocks throughout the day. Passing by their instrument and playing their new song is play for them. A sixteen-year-old needs a longer structured block of time, perhaps an hour or more.

6. Have music reference books, including a good music dictionary, handy. When your children hit snags because they do not understand a musical term or a composer's period of history, encourage them to look it up. Let no obstacles hinder them.

7. Even if you are not studying the Suzuki method, you can apply the philosophy. Encourage your child to listen to recordings of the literature that he or she is studying. They will learn that there are different interpretations. Their task is to create their *own* interpretation.

8. One of my favorite piano teachers used to say, "Never play a piece the same way twice. Create something new from it every time you play it." For older students, this is a new interpretation, a different shaping to the phrase, a new contrast. This is a mandate to be involved with the music creatively.

   I have applied the same principle to my preschool students. I ask their parents to vary their practice pieces by having the students:

   a. Create a story around the music. Bach's minuets can become celebrations of court dancing at kingdoms filled with kings, queens, knights, and dragons.

   b. Dramatize the story.

   c. Read books for inspiration. For example, I use Emilie Boon's *Peterkin Meets a Star* (Random House) when introducing the Twinkle Variations. In Boon's book, Peterkin befriends a star and takes him home. When the star becomes ill, Peterkin realizes that he must put the star back in the sky. When he does, the star becomes well and happy again. This story makes for a wonderful opportunity to play the Twinkles in major and minor keys. Aunt Rhody can be transposed to minor to create the somber mood for the death of the goose.

   d. Write lyrics.

e. Create movement.

f. Experiment with changing the tempo, dynamics, and articulation (staccato, legato).

g. Improvise by ornamenting the melody and changing the harmony.

h. Transpose the piece to other keys. Changing major to minor, and vice versa, is especially fun for changing the mood of a piece.

i. Have family members accompany with rhythm instruments and song (a simple "orchestration").

9. Be wary of one of the greatest pitfalls for parents and students: to demand perfection in recital performance and view anything less as failure. Here music making is the most analogous to life and teaches our children a critical lesson. It is not that we *make* mistakes (they are inevitable!) but *how* we recover from them. Do we persevere and not give up? Can we continue to make beautiful music after the mistakes? Can we focus on what we did right instead of what went wrong? These are the true goals.

## Motivating Children: Making Music Fun

Our first job is to create an environment in which our children will *want* to make music, in spite of the hard work. To accomplish this goal, make music part of your lifestyle.

Limiting music only to a slotted practice time is no different from attending Sunday school but seeing no application of faith during the week or learning to read at school and never celebrating a great work of literature at home. If there is no shared joy, there is little learning. If you are a musician, your practicing and involvement with music are models for your child. If you are not a musician, start learning an instrument, preferably your child's instrument! Sometimes this is the best incentive. Your child will be thrilled to be progressing ahead of you.

Fun music making is creative music making. Develop a repertoire of storytelling, creative dramatics, movement, art, and children's literature activities to accompany pieces being learned. Each will become a new adventure instead of "the same piece played over and over again."

Make music part of your family traditions. Play chamber music. Sing around the piano or with the guitar. Have different theme songs for different holidays. Listen to good music daily in your home. You may want to celebrate composers' birthdays by listening to their works and playing them. Serve a meal representative of the composer's country or that period of history. Even have cake, ice cream, and candles. Enjoy trips to the symphony and the ballet. Music events should be associated with happy times. Recitals and group classes should be followed by parties. If the teacher doesn't provide one, have family parties at home or go out to a favorite restaurant. Invite your relatives or friends to share the special event. I know one Suzuki program which celebrates all *Book I* recitals with ice cream sundaes, *Book II* recitals with pizza, *Book III* recitals with hamburgers, and so on. Group class activities can focus on holiday themes. Studied pieces can be transposed to minor for Halloween or improvised with silly surprises for April Fool's Day. Students can arrange Easter hymn or Christmas carol medleys based on their favorite tunes. Encourage your children to be involved with other children who enjoy music. This is critical in junior high and high school when peer acceptance is a compelling motivation.

The young child whose world is filled with joyous music experiences will want to make his own music, just as he wanted to dress himself and feed himself. Music will be a natural part of the child's world as it was natural to the great men of music.

The renowned composers did not grow up in a vacuum. Most of these great musicians were raised in musical homes and were first trained by their parents during early childhood. J. S. Bach came from *seven* generations of organists and cantors. In turn, he trained his children.

Mozart's father, an established musician, dedicated his life to teaching the boy clavier and violin, coaching his performances and overseeing his compositions. Schubert also received violin and piano training from his father. Haydn's parents were amateur musicians. They loved folk music, and his father played the harp. Haydn was to use many of these folk themes in his music. Beethoven's father and grandfather were town musicians.

Chopin's father was a flautist, and his mother was a singer. Brahms's father played the double bass at the municipal theater. Strauss's father was the first horn player of the Munich Hofoper. Vivaldi was the son of one of the leading violinists of St. Mark's Chapel. Stravinsky's father was a respected opera singer. The list goes on and on.

Our goal is not to produce Bachs, Mozarts, and Beethovens (though it could happen!) but to gift our children with their own love for music making. Our ultimate goal is to equip followers of Jesus Christ with a powerful tool for loving and worshiping God.

# INTERLUDE

Alleluia!

Praise God in his Temple on earth,
praise him in his temple in heaven,
praise him for his mighty achievements,
praise him for his transcendent greatness!

Praise him with blasts of the trumpet,
praise him with lyre and harp,
praise him with drums and dancing,
praise him with strings and reeds,
praise him with clashing cymbals,
praise him with clanging cymbals!
Let everything that breathes praise Yahweh!

Alleluia!

(Psalm 150,TJB)

# 9

# *SUMMARY: MUSIC EDUCATION CHECKLIST*

*David and all the Israelites were celebrating with all their might before God, with songs and with harps, lyres, tambourines, cymbals, and trumpets.*

1 Chronicles 13:8

 The checklist that follows will help you to direct and organize your child's music training.

## Infant/Toddler

Create home music environment through:

1. Listening experiences (folk songs, serious art music).

2. Enjoying live music.

3. Singing.

4. Rhythm instrument play.

5. Movement games.

## Preschool Years

1. Use own body as first instrument.

2. Continue building folk song repertoire and childhood chants.

3. Introduce Sol-fa.

4. Widen listening program to a variety of music genres.

5. Enroll in Dalcroze, Kodály, Orff-Schulwerk, or Suzuki group program (or employ similar techniques).

6. Encourage creative movement/drama and early arts experiences.

7. Provide accessible instruments (i.e., Orff-Schulwerk instruments) for improvisatory play.

8. Introduce interval and rhythm patterns (i.e., clapping name, foods, other familiar words). Play with contrasts (i.e., loud/soft, high/low). Encourage speech play.

9. If interested in beginning the Suzuki method, have child:
    a. Listen to *Suzuki Book I* recording.
    b. Hear different instruments to select one for study.

10. Create family "orchestrations."

## School-Age/Junior High

1. Teach the Biblical importance of music making.

2. Encourage private study on an instrument.

3. Encourage disciplined (and creative) practicing.

4. Introduce the instrument families.

5. Learn easier instruments such as the recorder, guitar, possibly other folk instruments.

6. Introduce keyboard skills, if studying another instrument.

7. Plan music history listening program representative of all periods.

8. Understand the music history of the literature the child is playing.

9. Establish musicianship skills.

10. Establish music reading skills.

11. Develop music theory/keyboard harmony understanding.

12. Develop analysis skills.

13. Develop skills in transposition, chord playing, and improvisation.

14. Enjoy creating own compositions.

15. Provide integrated arts experiences.

16. Understand arts history as a whole.

17. Encourage choir and/or band (orchestra) experience. Student should be comfortable singing or playing own part.

18. Provide group class experiences where the student can regularly play.

19. Include formal recital experiences.

20. Encourage family ensemble music making as part of life-style.

21. Attend arts events.

### Junior High School/High School (In addition to the above skills)

1. Stress fine musicianship.

2. Become a functional musician and become comfortable in a variety of styles and improvisation techniques.

3. Be able to sightread comfortably (sightsing).

4. Apply skills on instrument in social, relevant setting (i.e., orchestra, choir, church services, jazz group, etc.).

5. Become comfortable performing as soloist and in ensemble.

6. Possibly study secondary instrument.

7. Incorporate literature, languages, and history studies in arts background.

8. Possibly begin voice study.

9. Be involved with other young people who make music. Investigate summer music camps.

10. Fully develop music theory/eartraining skills and music history background.

11. Possibly investigate different careers in music. Remember that developing professional musicians was never the goal.

## Potential Church/Community School Program

1. Music/movement exploration sessions for infants/toddlers.

2. Preschool class based on knowledge of current music education methods.

3. Graded choir program.

4. Private consulting music teachers for instrument study.

5. Youth orchestra.

6. Creative arts summer program.

7. Group classes to teach comprehensive musicianship skills.

## Group Class Curriculum Checklist

These topics can be covered in a group class setting to supplement private lessons.

1. Music history listening program.
2. Sol-fa/sight singing.
3. Ensemble singing.
4. Exposure to instruments of the orchestra.
5. Instruction on recorder, guitar, other folk instruments.
6. Keyboard instruction (for nonpianists).
7. Music theory instruction, ear training.
8. Solo performance opportunities (in a variety of styles).
9. Ensemble performance opportunities (in a variety of styles).

## Special Curriculum

1. Integrated arts experience: movement, art, drama, music.
2. Dalcroze, Orff, Kodály, or Suzuki emphasis.

# MUSIC RESOURCES

## Introductory Music Books

Bernstein, Leonard. *The Joy of Music.* New York: Simon and Schuster, 1959.

Copland, Aaron. *What to Listen for in Music,* rev. ed. New York: McGraw-Hill, 1957.

Dallin, L. *Listener's Guide to Musical Understanding.* Dubuque, IA: W. C. Brown, 1977.

Machlis, Joseph. *The Enjoyment of Music,* 3d ed. New York: Norton, 1970.

## Music Reference Books

Ammer, C. *The A to Z of Foreign Musical Terms.* New York: Schirmer, 1989.

Apel, W. *Harvard Dictionary of Music.* Cambridge, MA: Harvard University Press, 1944.

Barlow, H. and S. Morgenstern. *A Dictionary of Musical Themes.* New York: Crown, 1948.

Dart, T. *The Interpretation of Music.* New York: Harper and Row, 1954.

Duckles, V. *Music Reference and Research Materials: Bibliography.* New York: Free Press, 1974.

Fling, R. M., ed. *A Basic Music Library: Essential Scores and Books.* Chicago, IL: American Library Association, 1983.

Gardner, J., ed. *Music; Cinema; Theater; The Novel; Painting; Opera; Architecture; Poetry; Dance.* Newsweek Books World of Culture Series. New York: Newsweek.

Grammand, P. *The Harmony Illustrated Encyclopedia of Classical Music.* New York: Harmony Books, 1988.

Grove, Sir George, ed. *Grove's Dictionary of Music and Musicians.* 9 vols. New York: St. Martin's, 1954.

Hindley, G. *The Larousse Encyclopedia of Music.* New York: World Publishing, 1971.

Osborne, C. *The Dictionary of Composers.* Taplinger Publications, 1981.

*The New Oxford Companion to Music.* London: Oxford University Press, 1983.

Pallay, S. G. *Cross-Index Title Guide to Classical Music.* Westport, CT: Greenwood, 1987.

Slonimsky, N., ed. *Baker's Biographical Dictionary of Musicians.* New York: Schimer, 1978.

Thompson, O. *International Cyclopedia of Music and Musicians.* New York: Dodd, Mead, 1975.

## Music History

Brockway, W. and H. Weinstock. *Men of Music.* New York: Simon and Schuster, 1958.

Brown, H. *Music in the Renaissance.* Englewood Cliffs, NJ: Prentice-Hall, 1976.

Bukofzer, Manfred. *Music in the Baroque Era.* New York: Norton, 1947.

Cobbett, W. *Cobbett's Cyclopedic Survey of Chamber Music.* New York: Oxford University Press, 1963.

Davison, A. and W. Apel, eds. *Historical Anthology of Music.* Cambridge, MA: Harvard University Press, 1949–50.

Grout, Donald J. *A History of Western Music,* rev. ed. New York: Norton, 1973.

———. *A Short History of Opera.* New York: Columbia University Press, 1965.

Hansen, Peter S. *An Introduction to Twentieth Century Music,* 3d ed. Boston: Allyn and Bacon, 1971.

Hitchcock, H. W. *Music in the United States: A Historical Introduction.* Englewood Cliffs, NJ: Prentice-Hall, 1969.

Hoppin, R. *Anthology of Medieval Music.*

———. *Medieval Music.* New York: Norton, 1978.

Klaus, Kenneth B. *The Romantic Period in Music.* Boston: Allyn and Bacon, 1970.

Lang, Paul H. *Music in Western Civilization.* New York: Norton, 1941.

Longyear, Rey M. *Nineteenth-Century Romanticism in Music.* Englewood Cliffs, NJ: Prentice-Hall, 1969.

Machlis, Joseph. *Introduction to Contemporary Music.* New York: Norton, 1961.

Mason, C., ed. *Oxford Studies of Composers.* New York: Oxford University Press, 1965.

Newman, William S. *The Sonata in the Classic Era.* New York: Norton, 1972.

Orrey, L., and G. Chase. *The Encyclopedia of Opera.* New York: Scribner, 1976.

Palisca, Claude V. *Baroque Music.* Englewood Cliffs, NJ: Prentice-Hall, 1968.

————. *Norton Anthology of Western Music.* 2 vols. New York: Norton, 1980.

Parrish, C., and J. Ohl. *Masterpieces of Music Before 1750.* New York: Norton, 1951.

Pauly, Reinhard G. *Music and the Theater: An Introduction to Opera.* Englewood Cliffs, NJ: Prentice-Hall, 1970.

————. *Music in the Classic Period,* 2d ed. Englewood Cliffs, NJ: Prentice-Hall, 1973.

Reese, Gustave. *Music in the Middle Ages.* New York: Norton, 1940.

Rosen, Charles. *The Classical Style: Haydn, Mozart, Beethoven.* New York: Norton, 1972.

Salzman, Eric. *Twentieth-Century Music: An Introduction.* Englewood Cliffs, NJ: Prentice-Hall, 1967.

Seay, Albert. *Music in the Medieval World.* Englewood Cliffs, NJ: Prentice-Hall, 1965.

Smith, J. S., and B. Carlson. *The Gift of Music, Great Composers and Their Influence.* Westchester, IL: Crossway Books, 1987.

Strunk, W. O. *Source Readings in Music History.* New York: Norton, 1950.

Ulrich, H. *Chamber Music.* New York: Columbia University Press, 1966.

————, and Paul Pisk. *A History of Music and Musical Style.* New York: Harcourt, Brace and World, 1963.

Watanabe, R. *Introduction to Music Research.* Englewood Cliffs, NJ: Prentice-Hall, 1970.

Westrup, J., ed. *The Master Musicians Series.* London: J. M. Dent, 1954.

————, ed. *The New Oxford History of Music.* New York: Oxford University Press, 1957.

Williams, M. *The Jazz Tradition.* New York: Oxford University Press, 1970.

## Music Theory

Christ, W., R. Delone, V. Kliewer, L. Rowell, and W. Thomson. *Materials and Structure of Music.* Englewood Cliffs, NJ: Prentice-Hall, 1972.

Dallin, Leon. *Foundations in Music Theory.* Belmont, CA: Wadsworth, 1967.

————. *Techniques of Twentieth-Century Composition* Dubuque, IA: W. C. Brown, 1974.

Evans, R. *How to Read Music.* New York: Crown, 1978.

Greer, D. *Form in Tonal Music.* New York: Holt, Reinhart, and Winston, 1965.

Hanshumaker, James, and J. Zorn. *Fundamentals: Learning Through Making Music.* Sherman Oaks, CA: Alfred, 1980.

————. *Fundamentals of Music Theory.* Englewood Cliffs, NJ: Prentice-Hall, 1987.

Harder, Paul. *Basic Materials in Music Theory.* Boston: Allyn and Bacon, 1970.

Kennan, K. *The Technique of Orchestration.* Englewood Cliffs, NJ: Prentice-Hall, 1970.

Kynaston, T., and R. Ricci. *Jazz Improvisation.* Englewood Cliffs, NJ: Prentice-Hall, 1978.

Nye, R., and B. Bjornar. *Basic Music.* Englewood, NJ: Prentice-Hall, 1987, for the non-music major.

Ottman, R. *Elementary Harmony.* Englewood Cliffs, NJ: Prentice-Hall, 1970.

———. *Music for Sight-Singing.* Englewood Cliffs, NJ: Prentice-Hall, 1967.

Piston, W. *Counterpoint.* New York: Norton, 1947.

———. *Harmony.* New York: Norton, 1962.

———. *Orchestration.* New York: Norton, 1955.

Watson, J. *Perspectives in Music Theory.* New York: Dodd, Mead, 1975.

## Music Education

Andress, B. *Promising Practices: Prekindergarten Music Education.* Reston, VA: MENC,* 1989.

Aronoff, F. *Music and Young Children.* New York: Turning Wheel Press, 1979.

Birge, E. B. *History of Public School Music in the U. S.* 1928, available from MENC.

Boswell, J. *The Young Child and Music: Contemporary Principles in Child Development and Music Education.* Reston, VA: MENC, 1985.

* MENC is: Music Education National Conference, Reston, VA.

*Careers in Music,* brochure. Reston, VA: MENC.

Choksy, et al. *Teaching Music in the 20th Century.* Englewood Cliffs, NJ: Prentice-Hall, 1986. Definitive text on Dalcroze, Orff, Kodály, and comprehensive musicianship.

Dewey, John. *Art as Experience.* New York: Minton, Balch and Co., 1934.

Gordon, E. *Learning Sequences in Music.* Chicago: GIA Publications, 1984.

————. *The Psychology of Music Teaching.* Englewood Cliffs, NJ: Prentice-Hall, 1971.

Landis, B. and P. Carder. *The Eclectic Curriculum in Music Education: Dalcroze, Kodály, and Orff.* Reston, VA: MENC, 1972.

Leonhard, C. and R. House. *Foundations and Principles of Music Education.* New York: McGraw-Hill, 1972.

Marsh, M. *Explore and Discover Music: Creative Approaches.* New York: Macmillan, 1970.

McDonald, D. T. *Musical Growth and Development: Birth Through Six.* New York: Schirmer, 1988.

"Major Approaches to Music Education: Kodály, Orff, Dalcroze, and Suzuki." *Music Educators Journal,* special issue, (February 1986).

Nash, Grace. *Creative Approaches to Child Development with Music, Language, and Movement.* Van Nuys, CA: Alfred, 1974.

Reimer, B. *A Philosophy of Music Education.* Englewood Cliffs, NJ: Prentice-Hall, 1989.

Ristad, E. *A Soprano on Her Head.* Moab, Utah: Real People Press, 1982.

Sheehy, E. D. *Children Discover Music and Dance.* New York: Teachers College Press, 1968.

Ward, J. *Careers in Music.* New York: H. Z. Walck, 1968.

Wilson, F. *Tone Deaf and All Thumbs? An Invitation to Music Making for Late Bloomers and Non-Prodigies.* New York: Penguin Press, l986.

## Dalcroze

Abramson, Robert. *Rhythm Games for Perception and Cognition.* Volkwein Bros., 1978.

Driver, Ethel. *A Pathway to Dalcroze Eurhythmics.* London: Thomas Nelson, 1963.

Findlay, Elsa. *Rhythm and Movement: Applications of Dalcroze Eurhythmics.* Princeton, NJ: Summy Birchard. 1971.

Jacques-Dalcroze, Emile. *Rhythm, Music, and Education.* London: Riverside Press, 1967.

Steinitz, T. *Teaching Music in Rhythmic Lessons: Theory and Practice of the Dalcroze Method.* Tel Aviv: OR-TAV Music Publications, 1988.

Vanderspar, E. *Dalcroze Handbook: Principles and Guidelines for Teaching Eurhythmics.*

Wax, Edith. *Dalcroze Dimensions.* Roslyn Heights, NY: Mostly Movement, Ltd.

———, and Sydell Roth. *Mostly Movement I: First Steps.* Roslyn Heights, NY: Mostly Movement, Ltd.

———. *Mostly Movement II: Accent on Autumn.* Roslyn Heights, NY: Mostly Movement, Ltd.

———. *Move with a Song.* Roslyn Heights, NY: Mostly Movement, Ltd.

## Kodály

Choksy, L. and Brummitt. *120 Singing Games and Dances.* New York: Prentice-Hall, 1987.

Choksy, Lois. *The Kodály Method.* Englewood Cliffs, NJ: Prentice-Hall, 1988.

Erdei, P. *150 American Folk Songs to Sing, Read and Play.*

Kaplan, B., ed. *The Kodály Concept.* Organization of American Kodály Educators, 1985.

Kersey, R. *Just Five.*

————. *Just Five Plus Two.*

Kodály, Zoltan. *The Selected Writings.* New York: Boosey and Hawkes, 1975.

Laszlo, E. *Zoltan Kodály: His Life and Work.* New York: Belwin Mills, 1972.

Szabo, H. *The Kodály Concept of Music Education.* New York: Boosey and Hawkes, 1968.

Szönyi, E. *Kodály's Principles in Practice.* London: Boosey and Hawkes, 1973.

## Orff-Schulwerk

Bitzon, C. *Alike and Different: The Clinical and Educational Use of Orff-Schulwerk.* Santa Ana, CA: Rosha Press, 1976.

Fuoco-Lawson, G. *Street Games.* St. Louis: MMB Music.

Gillespie, A. *Zing, Zing, Zing.*

————. *Hellos and Goodbyes.*

Keetman, Gunild. *Elementaria: First Acquaintance with Orff-Schulwerk,* trans. Margaret Murray. London: Schott and Co., Ltd., 1974.

Keller, Wilhelm. *Introduction to Music for Children: Methodology, Playing the Instruments, Suggestions for Teachers,* trans. Susan Kennedy. New York: Schott and Co., Ltd., 1974.

Leiss, Calder, and Boyas. *Carl Orff: His Life and Music.* London, 1966.

Orff, Carl, and Gunild Keetman. *Orff-Schulwerk: Music for Children,* ed. A. Doreen Hall and Arnold Walter. 5 vols. Mainz: B. Schott's Söhne. Also ed. B. Margaret Murray. 5 vols. London: Schott and Co., Ltd.

————. *The Schulwerk,* trans. Margaret Murray. New York: Schott Music Corp., 1978.

————. *Re-Echoes.* Cleveland, OH: American Orff-Schulwerk Association, 1977.

Stringham, Mary, comp. *Bibliography of Materials in English Concerning Orff-Schulwerk.* Cleveland, OH: American Orff-Schulwerk Association, 1977.

————, coll. and trans. *Orff-Schulwerk: Background and Commentary.* St. Louis: Magnamusic, 1976.

## Orff in the Church

McRae, Shirley. *Celebrate; Angel at the Door; Glow Ree Bee.*

Pringer, R. *Orff in the Church.*

Ramseth, Betty Ann. *Making Happy Noises; Open Thou Lips; Prepare Ye the Way; Take a Hymn; Hand-Me-Down Hymn.*

# Suzuki

Bigler, C., and V. Lloyd-Watts. *Studying Suzuki Piano: More Than Music*. Athens, OH: Ability Development, 1979.

Hermann, E. *Shinichi Suzuki: The Man and the Philosophy*. Athens, OH: Ability Development, 1981.

Honda, M. *Suzuki Changed My Life*. Princeton, NJ: Summy Birchard, 1984.

Kataoka. *Thoughts on the Suzuki Piano School*. Princeton, NJ: Birch Tree.

Kendall, J. *Suzuki Violin Method in American Music Education*. Princeton, NJ: Summy Birchard, 1984.

Landers, R. *The Talent Education School of Shinichi Suzuki: An Analysis*. Smithtown, NY: Exposition, 1980.

Mills, E., and T. Murphy, Sr. *The Suzuki Concept: An Introduction to a Successsful Method for Early Music Education*. Berkeley, CA: Diablo, 1973.

Mills, S. *In the Suzuki Style*. Berkeley, CA: Diablo, 1974.

Morris, C. *A Suzuki Parent's Diary*. Athens, OH: Ability Development, 1984.

Slone, K. *They're Rarely Too Old or Too Young to Twinkle*. Lexington, KY: Life Force, 1982.

Starr, W., and C. Starr. *To Learn with Love*. Knoxville, TN: Kingston Ellis, 1983.

Starr, W. *The Suzuki Violinist*. Knoxville, TN: Kingston Press, 1976.

Suzuki, Shinichi. *Ability Development from Age Zero,* trans. Mary Nagata. Athens, OH: Ability Development, 1981.

————. *Nurtured by Love: The Classic Approach to Talent Education,* trans. Waltraud Suzuki. Smithtown, NY: Exposition, 1973.

————. *Where Love Is Deep,* trans. Kyoka Selden. St. Louis: Talent Education Journal, 1982.

Thornton, A. *A Parent's Guide to the Suzuki Method.*

## Music Therapy/Psychology of Music

Alvin, J. *Music for Handicapped Children.* London: Oxford University Press, 1965.

Asmus, Edward, ed. *Proceedings of the Research Symposium on the Psychology and Acoustics of Music.* Lawrence, KS: University Press, 1978.

Bailey, P. *They Can Make Music.* London: Oxford University Press, 1973.

Bitcon, C. *Alike and Different: The Clinical and Educational Use of Orff-Schulwerk.* Santa Ana, CA: Rosha Press, 1976.

————. *Risk It . . . Express!* St. Louis: MMB Music, 1989.

Blacking, J. *How Musical Is Man?* Seattle, WA: University of Washington Press, 1973.

Bonny, H., and L. Savary. *Music and Your Mind.* New York: Harper and Row, 1973.

Bright, R. *Music in Geriatric Care.* New York: St. Martin's, 1972.

Campbell, D. *Introduction to the Musical Brain.* St. Louis: MMB Music, 1983.

Colwell, Richard. *The Evaluation of Music Teaching and Learning.* Englewood Cliffs, NJ: Prentice-Hall, 1970.

Critchley, MacDonald, and R. A. Henson. *Music and the Brain: Studies in the Neurology of Music.* Springfield, IL: Charles C. Thomas, 1977.

Davies, John B. *The Psychology of Music.* Stanford: Stanford University Press, 1978.

Dowling and Harwood. *Music Cognition.* Orlando, FL: Academic Press, 1986.

Eddy, J. *The Music Came from Deep Inside.* Brookline Books, 1989.

Edwards, E. *Music Education for the Deaf.* Meriam Edgar, 1974.

Evans and Clynes. *Rhythm in Psychological, Linguistic and Musical Processes.* Springfield, IL: Charles C. Thomas, 1986.

Farnsworth, Paul R. *The Social Psychology of Music.* Iowa City, IA: The University of Iowa Press, 1969.

Gaston, T. *Music in Therapy.* New York: MacMillan, 1968.

Graham, R. *Developmental Music Therapy.* KS: National Association for Music Therapy, 1975.

———. *Music for Special Learners,* 1985.

Green, B., and T. Gallwey. *The Inner Game of Music.* New York: Doubleday, 1986.

Hargreaves, D. *The Developmental Psychology of Music.* Cambridge: Cambridge University Press, 1986.

Hodges, Donald A., ed. *Handbook of Music Psychology.* KS: National Association for Music Therapy, 1980.

Lehman, Paul R. *Tests and Measurements in Music.* Englewood Cliffs, NJ: Prentice-Hall, 1968.

Lundin, Robert. *An Objective Psychology of Music*. New York: Ronald Press, 1967.

Madsen, Clifford, and Douglas Greer. *Research in Music Behavior*. New York: Teacher's College Press, 1975.

————, and Charles Madsen. *Experimental Research in Music*. Englewood Cliffs, NJ: Prentice-Hall, 1970.

Madsen and Prickett. *Applications of Research in Music Behavior*. St. Louis, MO: MMB Music.

"Music for the Exceptional Child." *Music Educators' Journal*, special issue, no. 68. 1982.

Nordoff, P., and Robbins. *Music Therapy in Special Education*. New York: John Day, 1971.

Orff, G. *The Orff Music Therapy*.

Peters, J. A. *Music Therapy—An Introduction*. Springfield, IL: Charles C. Thomas, 1987.

Phelps, Roger P. *A Guide to Research in Music Education*. Dubuque, IA: Wm. C. Brown, 1980.

Priestly, M. *Music Therapy in Action*. New York: St. Martin's, 1975.

Radocy, Rudolph E., and David J. Boyle. *Measurement and Evaluation of Musical Experience*. New York: Schirmer, 1987.

————. *Psychological Foundations of Musical Behavior*. Springfield, IL: Charles C. Thomas, 1979.

Roederer, Juan G. *Introduction to the Physics and Psychophysics of Music*. New York: Springer-Verlag, 1975.

Schulberg, C. *Music Therapy Sourcebook*. Human Sciences, 1981.

Shuter, Rosamund. *The Psychology of Musical Ability*. London: Butler and Tanner, Ltd.; U.S. Distributor: Barnes and Noble, Inc., 1968.

Sloboda, J. *The Musical Mind*. St. Louis, MO: MMB Music.

*The Use of the Creative Arts in Therapy*. Washington, D.C.: American Psychiatric Association, 1980.

Whybrew, W. E. *Measurement and Evaluation in Music*. Dubuque, IA: Wm. C. Brown, 1962.

## Instruments

Ardley, N. *Music*. New York: Knopf, 1989.

Arnold, C. R. *Organ Literature: A Comprehensive Survey*. Metuchen, NJ: Scarecrow Press, 1973.

Ben-tovim and Boyd. *The Right Instrument for Your Child: A Practical Guide*. Morrow Publications, 1986.

*Brass Anthology*. Evanston, IL: *Instrumentalist*, 1981.

Cook, G. D. *Teaching Percussion*. New York: Schirmer, 1988.

Diagram Group. *Musical Instruments of the World*. New York: Facts on File Publications, 1978.

Gill, D., ed. *Book of the Violin*. New York: Rizzoli, 1987.

Goodman, H. A. *Instrumental Music Guide*. Provo, UT: Brigham Young University Press, 1977.

Kendall, A. *The World of Musical Instruments*. London: Hamlyn Publications, 1972.

Klotman, R. H. *Teaching Strings*. New York: Schirmer, 1988.

Marcuse, S. *Musical Instruments: A Comprehensive Dictionary*. New York: Norton, 1975.

Music Educators National Conference. *The Complete String Guide*. Reston, VA: MENC, 1988.

W. W. Norton Series: Books That Live in Music. New York: 1970s.

Baines, A. *Woodwind Instruments and Their History*.

Bate, P. *The Flute*.

———. *The Oboe*.

———. *The Trumpet and Trombone*.

Langwill, L. G. *The Bassoon and Contrabassoon*.

Morley-Pezze, R. *The French Horn*.

Nelson. *The Violin and Viola*.

Rendall, R. *The Clarinet*.

Pellerite, J. *A Handbook of Literature for the Flute*. Bloomington, IN: Zalo Publications.

Rensch, R. *The Harp: Its History, Technique and Repertoire*. London: Duckworth, 1969.

———. *Harps and Harpists*. Indiana University Press, 1989.

Russell, R. *Harpsichord and Clavichord*. New York: Schirmer, 1981.

Stevens, R. *Artistic Flute Technique and Study*. Hollywood, CA: Highland Music.

Stimpson, M. *The Guitar: A Guide for Students and Teachers*. Oxford: Oxford University Press, 1988.

Sumner, W. *The Organ*. New York: St. Martin's, 1978.

Whitener, S. *A Complete Guide to Brass*. New York: Schirmer, 1989.

Winternitz, E. *Musical Instruments of the Western World*. New York: McGraw-Hill, 1967.

*Woodwind Anthology.* Evanston, IL: *Instrumentalist,* 1980.

## Piano

Adler, K. *The Art of Accompanying and Coaching.* New York: DeCapo Bess, 1965.

Bastien, J. *How to Teach Piano Successfully.* Park Ridge, IL: General Words and Music, 1977. Includes a complete bibliography on piano pedagogy, history, and literature.

Fine, L. *The Piano Book: Guide to Buying a New or Used Piano.* MA: Brookside, 1987.

Friskin, J., and I. Freundlich. *Music for the Piano.* New York: Dover, 1973.

Gillespie, J. *Five Centuries of Keyboard Music.* New York: Dover, 1972.

Hinson, M. *Guide to the Pianist's Repertoire,* vols. 1 and 2. Bloomington: Indiana University Press, 1977.

————. *Piano Teacher's Source Book.* Melville, NY: Belwin Mills, 1980.

Musafia, J. *The Art of Fingering in Piano Playing.* New York: Music Corporation of America, 1972.

## Music and Worship

Allen, R. B. *Lord of Song.* Portland, OR: Multnomah, 1985.

————, and G. Borror. *Worship, Rediscovering the Missing Jewel.* Portland, OR: Multnomah, 1982.

Berglund, R. *A Philosophy of Church Music.* Chicago: Moody, 1985.

Blume, F. *Protestant Church Music*. New York: W. W. Norton, 1974.

Hayford, J. W. *Worship His Majesty*. Waco, TX: Word, 1987.

Hustad, D. *Jubilate!* Carol Stream, IL: Hope, 1981.

Lovelace and Rice. *Music and Worship in the Church*. Nashville, TN: Abingdon Press, 1976.

Martin, R. *The Worship of God*. Grand Rapids, MI: Eerdmans, 1982.

————. *Worship in the Early Church*. Grand Rapids, MI: Eerdmans, 1964.

Ortlund, A. *Up with Worship*. Ventura, CA: Regal, 1975.

Osbeck, K. W. *Singing with Understanding*. Grand Rapids: Kregel 1979, also *101 Hymn Stories*.

Parker, A. *Creative Hymn-Singing*. Chapel Hill, NC: Hinshaw Music, 1976.

Routley, E. *Church Music and the Christian Faith*. Carol Stream, IL: Agape, 1978, also *Words, Music and the Church*.

Webber, R. E. *Worship, Old and New*. Grand Rapids, MI: Zondervan, 1982.

## Voice/Choral

Caruso, E. and L. Tetrazzini. *The Art of Singing*. New York: Dover, 1975.

Colorni, E. *Singer's Italian*. New York: Schirmer, 1970.

Cox, R. *The Singer's Manual of German and French Diction*. New York: Schirmer, 1970.

Decker, H., and J. Herford. *Choral Conducting: A Symposium*. Englewood Cliffs, NJ: Prentice-Hall, 1973.

Espina, N. *Repertoire for the Solo Voice*. Metuchen, NJ: Scarecrow Press, 1977.

Finn, William. *The Art of the Choral Conductor*. Evanston, IL: Summy-Birchard, 1960.

Gordon, L. *Choral Director's Complete Handbook*. West Nyack, NY: Parker Publishing, 1977.

Heffernan, C. *Choral Music: Technique and Artistry*. Englewood Cliffs, NJ: Prentice-Hall, 1982.

Henderson, L. *How to Train Singers*. West Nyack, NY: Parker Publishing, 1979.

Kagen, S. *Music for the Voice*. Bloomington: Indiana University Press, 1968.

May, W., and C. Tolin. *Pronunciation Guide for Choral Literature*. Reston, VA: MENC, 1987.

Miller, R. *The Structure of Singing*. New York: Schirmer, 1986.

Robinson, R., and A. Winold. *The Choral Experience: Literature, Materials, and Methods*. New York: Harper and Row, 1976.

Robinson, R., ed. *Choral Music*. New York: Norton, 1978.

Schmidt, J. *Basis of Singing*. New York: Schirmer, 1989.

Swears, Linda. *Teaching the Elementary School Chorus*. West Nyack, NY: Parker, 1988.

Ulrich, H. *A Survey of Choral Music*. New York: Harcourt Brace Jovanovich, 1973.

Vennard, William. *Singing, the Mechanism and Technique*. New York: Carl Fischer, 1967.

Wienandt, E. *Choral Music of the Church.* New York: DaCapo, 1980.

Young, P. M. *The Choral Tradition.* New York: Norton, 1981.

## Music Services for the Blind*

American Printing House for the Blind
    1839 Frankfort Avenue
    P. O. Box 6085
    Louisville, KY 40206

National Library Service for the Blind and Physically Handicapped
    Library of Congress
    Washington, D.C. 20542
    (Publishes *The Musical Mainstream*)

National Braille Association
    422 Clinton Avenue South
    Rochester, NY 14620

## Braille Music Books

DeGarmo, Mary. *Introduction to Braille Music Transcription.* Washington, DC: Library of Congress, 1970.

Jenkins, E. *Primer of Braille Music.* Louisville, KY: American Printing House for the Blind, 1960.

Krolick, B. *Dictionary of Braille Music Signs.* Washington, DC: Library of Congress, 1979.

————. *How to Read Braille Music.* Champaign, IL: Stipes, 1975.

---

* Braille music available

# CHILDREN'S MUSIC RESOURCES

## Children's Music Books

Cassatt, M. *Lullabies and Good Night.*

Feierabend, John. *Music for Very Little People.*

Gelineau, R. Phyllis. *Songs in Action.*

Gillespie, A. *Zing, Zing, Zing; Hellos and Goodbyes.*

Glazer, T. *Music for Ones and Twos; Do Your Ears Hang Low? Eye Winker, Tom Tinker, Chin Chopper; Treasury of Songs for Children.*

Hoermann and Bridges. *Catch a Song.*

Jennings, P., and T. Jennings. *Big Round Book.*

Jenkins, Ella. *Ella Jenkins Songbook.*

Jones, Bessie. *Step it Down.*

Kersey, R. *Just Five.* and *Just Five Plus Two*

Kirkland and Han. *Pocketbook of Rounds.*

Lomax, A. *Folk Songs of North America.*

Luboff, N. *International Book of Folk Songs*.

Lynn, Frank. *Songs for Swingin' Housemothers*.

Metropolitan Museum of Art. *Go In and Out the Window*.

McCrae, S. *Sing 'Round the World*.

Nash, G., and J. Rapley. *Holidays and Special Days*.

Nelson, Esther. *The Great Rounds Songbook; The Best Singing Games; Dancing Games for Children; The Funny Song Book; The Silly Song Book; Musical Games for Children of All Ages; Holiday Singing and Dancing Games*.

*The New Illustrated Disney Songbook*. New York: Harry Abrams, 1986.

Palmer, Hap. *Hap Palmer Favorites*.

Raffi. *The Raffi Singable Songbook; The Second Raffi Songbook; Everything Grows; Christmas Treasury*.

Seeger, R. *American Folk Songs for Children*.

Vogel, A. *The Big Book for Little Singers*. Muenster, Germany: Coppenrath Verlag, 1987.

Watson, C. *Father Fox's Feast of Songs*. New York: Philomel, 1983.

Wee Sing Series—tape and songbook sets, Los Angeles, CA: Price, Stern, and Sloan, Volumes: *Wee Sing; Wee Sing and Play; Wee Sing Silly Songs; Wee Sing Nursery Rhymes and Lullabyes; Wee Sing Around the Campfire; Wee Sing Bible Songs; Wee Sing for Christmas; Wee Sing America*.

Weiss, N. *If You're Happy and You Know It: Story Songs*. New York: Greenwillow, 1987.

Wessells, K. *The Golden Songbook*. New York: Golden Press, 1981.

Winn, M., ed. *The Fireside Book of Children's Songs*. New York: Simon and Schuster, 1966.

## Music Theory Programs for Children*

Lennon, R. D. *Keyboard Capers*. Knoxville, TN: Elijah, 1986.

Yurko, M. *No H in Snake*. Sherman Oaks, CA: Alfred, 1979.

## Music Games and Aids for Children

Available from Jensen Publications: Lavender, Cheryl. *Composer Bingo; Instrument Bingo; Rhythm Bingo*.

Available from Music in Motion: *Music Crosswords, Mazes and Puzzles; Music Bingo; Music's My Bag;* (includes giant staff); *Music Maestro; The Great Composers Game; Forward March, Dominoes*.

Available from Music 19 (Michiko Yurko): *Musopoly; Have a Great Recital; Perfectly Silly Perfect Practicing Game*.

Parkin, M. C. *Mommy, Can We Practice Now?* games and activities.

## Music History Books for Children

*Barron's Educational Series on Composers and Artists*. Barron's Publishing, 250 Wireless Blvd., Hauppauge, New York 11788.

Bernstein, L. *Young People's Concerts*. New York: Simon and Schuster, 1970.

Britten, B., and Imogen Holst. *The Wonderful World of Music*. Garden City, New York: Doubleday, 1968.

---

* Most good instrument methods have accompanying theory books.

Cavendish, Marshall. *A Guide to Classical Music*. New York, 1987.

Dowley, T., and A. Orza. *The Illustrated Lives of the Great Composers Series*. Available from Music in Motion.

Goffstein, M. *A Little Schubert—Welcome to Music*. New York: Harper and Row. 1985.

Johnson, A. D. *The Value of Giving: The Story of Beethoven*. La Jolla, CA: Value Communications, 1979.

Kendall, C. *Stories of Composers for Young Musicians*. Toadwood Publ., 1982, also *More Stories of Composers*.

Ladybird History of the Arts Series: *History of Musical Instruments; Lives of the Great Composers; The Story of Music; The Story of the Ballet; The Story of the Theatre*.

*Musical Books for Young People Series*. Minneapolis, MN: Lerner Publications.

Available from Music in Motion: *Opera Funtime Books,* introducing children to the opera, and introductory ballet stories.

Novello. *Short Musical Biographies*. Fifteen-composer set.

Oxford First Companion Series: *Composers and Their Music; The Story of Music; Instruments and Orchestras; Singing and Dancing; Oxford Jr. Companion to Music*.

Rosenberg, J. *Sing Me a Story: The Metropolitan Opera's Book of Opera Stories for Children*. New York: Thames and Hudson, 1989.

Ventura, P. *Great Composers*. New York: GP Putnam, 1988.

Westberg, J. *The Pantheon Story of Music for Young People*. New York: Pantheon, 1968.

## Fun Books About Music for Children

Cosgrove, S. *Fiddler*. Portland, OR: Multnomah Press, 1987.

Elliott, D. *Alligators and Music*. Boston, MA: Harvard Common Press, 1976.

Kampen, V., and I. Eugen. *Orchestranimals*. New York: Scholastic Inc., 1989.

Kuskin, K. *The Philharmonic Gets Dressed*. New York: Harper and Row, 1982.

Meyrick, K. *The Musical Life of Gustav Mole*. Child's Play, 1989.

Micucci. *A Little Night Music*. New York: Morrow Books, 1989.

Staines, B. *All God's Critters Got a Place in the Choir*. Dutton, 1989.

Thacher, H. *Mama Don't Allow*. New York: Harper and Row, 1984.

Tusa, T. *Miranda*. New York: Aladdin, 1986.

Williams, V. *Music, Music for Everyone*. New York: Mulberry Books, 1984.

Also see: Bunker, P. "A Bibliography of Picture Books Inspired by Folk Songs." *Orff Echo*. 22, no. 3, (Spring 1990).

## Videos

*The Joy of Bach*. Vision Videos, 2030 Wentz Church Road, Worcester, PA 19490.

Menuhin, Yehudi. *The Music of Man Series*. Eight tapes covering all historical periods.

Mineria Symphony Orchestra. *The World's Greatest Music*. Videotape and Teacher's Guide available from MENC.

Royal Philharmonic Orchestra of London. *Discovering the Orchestra,* 5 tape series Boca Raton, FL: Social Issue Resource Series.

Royal Philharmonic conducted by Andre Previn. *Story of the Symphony.* BBC Series. Set of six composer tapes.

Saint-Saens. *Carnival of the Animals.* Twin Tower Enterprises.

Also available from Music in Motion: *History of Art and Music Series* (Covers the art and music of each historical period), *Instruments of the Symphony Orchestra, Great Composers and Their Music,* and *The Maestro's Company.* Write to them for their complete catalogue.

## Children's Educational Tapes/Records

Britten, Benjamin. *Young Person's Guide to the Orchestra.*

*The Instruments of the Orchestra.* Simon Says.

*Meet the Classics.* Sine Qua Non, 1983.

*Music and Life of Composers.* The Music Masters Series Richardson, TX: Cornerstone Curriculum Project.

*My First Concert.* Rochester Philharmonic Orchestra, 1985.

*The Orchestra.* Gateway, 1977.

*Stories of the Great Composers.* Gateway.

Rubin, M., and P. Ustinov, and the Toronto Philarmonia Orchestra. *The Orchestra*—book and tape. Available from Montessori Services, Santa Rosa, CA.

*Sounds of the World Series.* Reston, VA: MENC.

---

# CREATIVE ARTS RESOURCES

## Art History/Technique

Arnason, H. H. *History of Modern Art*. Englewood Cliffs, NJ: Prentice-Hall, 1977.

Art Journals: *The American Art Journal; Design for Arts in Education; Arts News; The Artists' Magazine; Art in America*.

Artist's Library Series. Tustin, CA: Walter Foster Publications.

Glassford, C. *Pen and Ink*.

Light, D. *Watercolor*.

Palluth, William. *Painting in Oils*.

Powell, William. *The World of Color and How to Use It*.

Bernard, C. *An Artist's Notebook, Techniques and Materials*. New York: Holt, Rinehart, and Winston, 1979.

Black, M. *New Key to Weaving*. New York: MacMillan, 1957.

David, L. *Design Basics*. New York: Holt, Rinehart, and Winston, 1979.

de la Croix, Horst, and R. G. Tansey. *Art Through the Ages.* New York: Harcourt Brace Jovanovich, 1975.

Fabri, F. *Color: A Complete Guide.* New York: Watson-Guptill, 1967.

Janson, H. W. *History of Art.* Englewood Cliffs, NJ: Prentice-Hall, 1962.

Karwoski, R. C. *Watercolor Bright and Beautiful.* New York: Watson-Guptill, 1988.

Keller, Horst. *The Great Book of French Impressionism.* New York: Greenwich House, 1975.

Nicolaides, K. *The Natural Way to Draw.* Boston: Houghton Mifflin, 1975.

O'Brien, V. *Techniques of Stained Glass.* Berkshire, England: Van Nostrand Reinhold, 1982.

*The Oxford Companion to Art.* New York: Oxford University Press, 1970.

Pile, J. *Interior Design.* New York: Abrams, 1988.

Smith, Ray. *The Artist's Handbook.* New York: Random House, 1988.

Taubes, F. *Acrylic Painting for the Beginner.* New York: Watson-Guptill, 1971.

Vasari, Giorgio. *The Great Masters.* New York: Park Lane, 1986.

## Art Education/Therapy

Arnheim, Rudolf. *Art and Visual Perception.* Berkeley: University of California Press, 1974.

Brookes, M. *Drawing with Children*. Los Angeles: Jeremy P. Tarcher, 1986.

Edwards, Betty. *Drawing on the Artist Within*. New York: Simon and Schuster, 1986.

————. *Drawing on the Right Side of the Brain*. Los Angeles: Jeremy P. Tarcher, 1979.

Frank, M. *I Can Make a Rainbow*. Nashville, TN: Incentive, 1976.

Kellogg, Rhoda. *Analyzing Children's Art*. Palo Alto, CA: National Press, 1969.

Kramer, Edith. *Childhood and Art Therapy*. New York: Schocken, 1979.

Naumberg, Margaret. *Dynamically Oriented Art Therapy*. New York: Gruner and Stratton, 1966.

Rhyne, Janie. *The Gestalt Art Experience*. CA: Wadsworth, 1973.

Uhlin, Donald M. *Art for Exceptional Children*. Dubuque, IA: William C. Brown, 1972.

Ulman, Elinor, and Penny Dachinger. *Art Therapy in Theory and Practice*. New York: Schocken, 1975.

## Dance History/Technique

Anderson, Jack. *Dance*. New York: Newsweek Books, 1974.

Balanchine, G. *George Balanchine's Complete Stories of the Great Ballet*. Garden City, New York: Doubleday, 1968.

Chujoy, A., and Manchester. *The Dance Encyclopedia*. New York: Simon and Shuster, 1967.

Jowitt, D. *Time and the Dancing Image.* Morrow Publications: 1987.

Kraus, R. *History of the Dance.* Englewood Cliffs, NJ: Prentice-Hall, 1967.

Liechtenhan, R. *From Dance to Ballet: An Illustrated History of Dance.* New York: Kraus Publishing, 1983.

Sorell, W. *The Dance Through the Ages.* New York: Grosset and Dunlap, 1967.

Stuart, M., and L. Kirstein. *The Classic Ballet.* New York: Knopf, 1972.

Walter, T. *The Ballet Companion: A Guide for the Ballet-Goer.* New York: Dodd, Mead, 1968.

Whitehill, A., and William Noble. *The Parents' Book of Ballet.* Colorado Springs, CO: Merriwether Publishing, 1988.

Also see *Dance Magazine.*

## Dance Education/Therapy

Barlin, Anne L., and Tamara R Greenberg. *Move and Be Moved.* Los Angeles: Learning Through Movement, 1980.

Bernstein, Penny Lewis. *Theory and Methods in Dance-Movement Therapy.* Dubuque, IA: Kendall and Hunt, 1972.

Canner, Norma. *And a Time to Dance.* Boston: Beacon, 1968.

Costonis, M. N. *Therapy in Motion.* Chicago: University of Illinois Press, 1978.

Doray, Maya. *J Is for Jump!* Fearon Teacher Aids, Pitman Learning, Inc.

Fleming, G. *Creative Rhythmic Movement.* Englewood Cliffs, NJ: Prentice-Hall, 1976.

Haselbach, B. *Dance Education*. London: Shott, 1978.

Hay, D., and D. Rogers. *Moving Through the Universe in Bare Feet: Ten Circle Dances*. Chicago: Swallow, 1974.

Joyce, M. *First Steps in Teaching Creative Dance to Children*. Palo Alto, CA: National Press.

Kokaska, S. *Creative Movement for Special Education*. Fearon Publications, 1974.

Lefco, Helene. *Dance Therapy*. Chicago: Nelson-Hall, 1974.

Mason, Kathleen C., ed. *Focus on Dance VII: Dance Therapy*. Washington, DC: American Alliance for Health, Physical Education, and Recreation, 1977.

Monsour, S., M. Cohen, and P. Lindell. *Rhythm in Music and Dance for Children*. Belmont, CA: Wadsworth, 1966.

Murray, R. *Dance in Elementary Education*. New York: Harper and Row, 1965.

Schoop, Trudi. *Won't You Join the Dance?* Palo Alto, CA: National Press, 1974.

Sullivan, Molly. *Movement Exploration for Young Children*. Washington, DC: National Association for the Education of Young Children, 1982.

Weikart, P. *Teaching Movement and Dance*. Yipsilanti, MI: High Scope, 1982, also *Round the Circle*.

Wethered, Audrey. *Movement and Drama in Therapy*. Boston, MA: Publishers-Plays, 1973.

## Drama Education/Therapy

Greenberg, Ira A., ed. *Psychodrama: Theory and Therapy*. New York: Behavioral Publications, 1974.

Jennings, Sue. *Remedial Drama*. New York: Theatre Arts Books, 1974.

McCaslin, Nellie. *Creative Dramatics in the Classroom*. New York: David McKay, 1968.

Philpott, A. R., ed. *Puppets and Therapy*. Boston: Plays, Inc., 1977.

Siks, Geraldine Brain. *Creative Dramatics, an Art for Children*. New York: Harper Brothers, 1958.

Slade, Peter. *Child Drama*. London: Hodder and Stoughton, 1954.

Spolin, Viola. *Improvisation for the Theater: Theater Games*. Evanston, IL: Northern Illinois Press, 1963.

Wagner, Betty Jane. *Dorothy Heathcote: Drama as a Learning Medium*. Washington, DC: National Education Association, 1976.

Ward, Winifred. *Playmaking with Children*. New York: D. Appleton-Century, 1947.

Way, Brian. *Development Through Drama*. New York: Humanities Press, 1967.

## General Arts Books

Billington, M. *Performing Arts: A Guide to Practice and Appreciation*. New York: Facts on File, 1980.

Brown, C., ed. *The Reader's Companion to World Literature*. New York: Mentor Books, 1973.

Fleming, William. *Art, Music, and Ideas*. New York: Holt, Rinehart, and Winston, 1970.

Hilton, Wendy. *Dance and Music*. Pendragon Series. Stuyvesant, New York: Pendragon Press.

Janson, H., and J. Kerman. *A History of Art and Music*. Englewood Cliffs, NJ: Prentice-Hall, 1968.

Waldhorn, A., O. Weber, and A. Zeiger. *Good Reading*. New York: Mentor Books, 1985. Definitive guide to literature, including the major books on all topics.

# CHILDREN'S BOOKS ON ART AND DANCE

## Children's Books on Art

*Barron's Educational Series on Artists and Composers.* 250 Wireless Blvd., Hauppauge, New York.

Brown, L. *Visiting the Art Museum.* New York: Dutton, 1986.

Goffstein, M. *An Artist—Welcome to Art.* New York: Harper and Row, 1980.

*History of Art for Young People.* New York: Abrams, 1987.

Janson, H. and A. Janson. *The History of Art for Young People.* New York: Abrams, 1987.

*Ladybird Series: Great Artists Series.*

Raboff, Ernest. *Art for Children.* New York: Harper and Row. Sixteen-volume series on the life and works of sixteen master artists.

Rothenstein, J., ed. *The Great Artists. A Library of Their Lives, Times and Painting.* 25 vols. New York: Funk and Wagnalls, 1978.

*Teach Art with the Masters.* Art Extension Press, P. O. Box 389, Westport, CT 06881.

*Usborne Guide to Drawing.* London: Usborne-Haynes Publishers, 1981.

*Usborne Guide to Painting* London: Usborne-Haynes Publishers, 1981.

*Usborne Story of Painting.* London: Usborne-Haynes Publishers, 1980.

Venezia, M. *Getting to Know the World's Greatest Artists Series.* Chicago: Childrens Press, 1988.

Ventura, P. *Great Painters.* Putnam, 1984.

Wolf, Aline. *Mommy, It's a Renoir.* Manual and postcard sets.


## Children's Books on Dance

DeMille, A. *To a Young Dancer.* Boston: Little, Brown, 1962.

Krementy, Jill. *The Very Young Dancer.* New York: Random House, 1976.

Rosenberg, J. *Dance Me a Story: Twelve Tales from the Classic Ballets.* New York: Thames and Hudson, 1985.

Thwaites, Lyndsay. *Rosie's Wonderful Dances.* London: Andre Duetsh, Ltd.

Vogel, Antje. *The Big Book for Little Dancers.* Muenster, Germany: Coppenrath Verlag, 1984.


## Dance Videos*

Baryshnikov: *The Dancers and the Dance*

---

\* Available from The Music Stand.

*The Ballet Workout*

*Video Dictionary of Classical Ballet*

David Howard: *Ballet Class*
      a. *Beginners*
      b. *Intermediate—Advanced*

*Dance Lessons for Children*
      a. *Ballet for Preschoolers*
      b. *Tap for Preschoolers*
      c. *Creative Dance for Preschoolers*
      d. *Jazz for Age 6-11*
      e. *Ballet for Age 6-11*
      f. *Tap for Age 6-11*

# GENERAL ART, MUSIC, AND POETRY RE-SOURCES FOR CHILDREN

Metropolitan Museum of Art. *Go In and Out the Window*. New York: Henry Holt and Co., 1987. Illustrated songbook.

Metropolitan Museum of Art. *Talking to the Sun*. New York: Henry Holt and Co., 1985. Illustrated anthology of poems.

Regniers, B. B. *Sing a Song of Popcorn: Anthology of Poetry*. New York: Scholastic, 1988.

Vergés, G. and O. Vergés. *Journey Through History Series*. New York: Barron's Educational Series, 1988.

# MUSIC ORGANIZATIONS AND JOURNALS

## Music Organizations

American Choral Directors Association
P. O. Box 6310
Lawton, OK 73506
(Publishes *The Choral Journal*)

American Harp Society
P. O. Box 38334
Los Angeles, CA 90038
(Publishes *American Harp Journal*)

American Musical Instrument Society
The Shrine to Music Museum
414 East Clark
Vermillion, SD 57069

American Musicological Society
201 South 34th Street
Philadelphia, PA 19104
(Publishes *Journal of the American Musicological Society*)

American Orff-Schulwerk Association
  P. O. Box 391089
  Cleveland, OH 44139–1089
  (Publishes *The Orff Echo*)

American Recorder Society
  596 Broadway #902
  New York, NY 10012
  (Publishes *The American Recorder*)

The American String Teachers Association
  UGA Station
  P. O. Box 2066
  Athens, GA 30612
  (Publishes *American String Teacher*)

Chamber Music America
  545 8th Avenue
  New York, NY
  (Publishes *Chamber Music Magazine*)

Dalcroze Society of America
  School of Music
  Duquesne University
  Pittsburgh, PA 15282
  (Publishes *The Dalcroze Journal* )

International Clarinet Society
  John Mohler, President
  School of Music
  University of Michigan
  Ann Arbor, MI 48109

International Double Reed Society
  Charles Veazey, President
  Lowry Riggins, Treasurer
  626 Lakeshore Drive
  Monroe, LA 71203

International Horn Society
    Ellen Powley, Executive Secretary
    2220 North 1400 E.
    Provo, UT 84606

International Society of Folk Harpers
    4718 Maychelle Dr.
    Anaheim, CA 92807-3040
    (Publishes *Folk Harp Journal*)

International Trombone Association
    Vern Kagarice
    School of Music
    University of North Texas
    Denton, TX 76203

International Trumpet Guild
    Bryan Goff, Treasurer
    School of Music
    Florida State University
    Tallahassee, FL 32306

Music Educators National Conference
    1902 Association Drive
    Reston, VA 22091
    (Publishes *Music Educators Journal,*
    *The Journal of Research in Music Education*)

Music Teachers National Association
    Robert Elias, Director
    617 Vine Street, Suite 1432
    Cincinnati, OH 45202

National Association of College Wind and Percussion Instruments
    Richard Weerts
    Northeast Missouri State University
    Kirksville, MO 63501

National Association for Music Therapy
    505 Eleventh Street, S.E.
    Washington, D.C. 20003
    (Publishes *Journal of Music Therapy,*
    *Music Therapy Perspectives)*

National Flute Association
    Ms. Myrna Brown
    805 Laguna Drive
    Denton, TX 76201
    (Publishes *The Flutist's Quarterly)*

National Guild of Piano Teachers
    American College of Musicians
    P. O. Box 1807
    Austin, TX 78767

The North American Saxophone Alliance
    Kenneth M. Fischer, President
    School of Music
    The University of Georgia
    Athens, GA 30602

Organization of American Kodály Educators
    James Fields
    Department of Music
    Box 2017
    Nicholls State University
    Thibodaux, LA 70301

The Percussive Arts Society
    James Lambert, Executive Editor
    Cameron University
    Box 16395
    Lawton, OK 74505

Richards Institute (Education Through Music)
   P. O. BOX 6249
   Bozeman, MT 59771-6249

Suzuki Association of the Americas
   P. O. Box 354
   Muscatin, IA 52761
   (Publishes *American Suzuki Journal*)

Tubist Universal Brotherhood Association
   School of Music
   Florida State University
   Tallahassee, FL 32306

Violoncello Society
   340 West 55th Street, Suite 5D
   New York, NY

## Other Music Journals

*Bulletin of the National Association of Teachers of Singing*

*Clavier**

*Flute Talk*†

*High Fidelity/Musical America*

*The Instrumentalist*‡

*Journal of Music Theory*

*Journal of the Violin Society of America*

*Musical Quarterly*

*Piano Quarterly*

---

* Published by Instrumentalist, 200 Northfield Road, Northfield, IL 60093.
† Ibid.
‡ Ibid.

*Woodwind—Brass and Percussion*

## Information Sources

Music Library Association
  Chicago, IL

Musicdata, Inc.
  Philadelphia, PA

National Music Publishers' Association
  New York, NY

Shipley, L. *Information Resources in the Arts: A Directory.* National Referral Service, Washington, DC: Library of Congress, 1986. (For a complete guide to arts organizations)

---

# *MUSIC COMPANIES*

The following companies will each send a comprehensive catalog at your request. Most music companies also carry records and tapes.

New resources are constantly coming out. Being on the mailing lists of these companies and professional organizations will keep you current on new products.

## Suzuki Companies

Ability Development
   Box 4260
   Athens, OH 45701-4260

Harnes-Selway Creative Arts Program
   2128 McKay Street
   Falls Church, VA 22043

Ithaca Talent Education
   929 Danby Road
   Box 669
   Ithaca, NY 14851

Kentuckiana Music Supply
   P. O. Box 14124
   Louisville, KY 40214

Twinkle Tree
   Foxes Music Company
   809 West Broad Street
   Falls Church, VA 22046

Young Musicians
   P. O. Box 48036
   Ft. Worth, TX 76148


## Music and Art Materials

Michael Olaf
   The Montessori Shop
   5817 College Avenue
   Oakland, CA 94618

Montessori Services
   228 South A Street
   Santa Rosa, CA 95401

Museum of Fine Arts (catalog)
   P. O. Box 1044
   Boston, MA 02120


## Music and Dance Resources

The Music Stand
   One Rockdale Plaza
   Lebanon, NH 03766

## Orff Books and Music

Shott Music Publishers
European-American Music Distributors
P. O. Box 850
Valley Forge, PA 19482-9985

## Music and Books*

Children's Book and Music Center
2500 Santa Monica Boulevard
Santa Monica, CA 90404

The Enchanted Workshop
2026 Gurney CT
Burlington, NC 27215

Friendship House
29313 Clemons Rd #2-G
P.O. Box 450978
Cleveland, OH 44145-0623

Jenson Publications
Music for Growing Minds Catalog
Music First Express
2770 South 171st Street
P. O. Box 248-M
New Berlin, WI 53151-0248

MMB Music (creative arts therapy materials)
10370 Page Industrial Blvd.
St. Louis, MO 63132

Music in Motion
109 Spanish Village, Suite 645
Dallas, TX 75248 (Music, books, and novelties—most comprehensive catalog available)

---

* Includes Orff, Dalcroze and Kodály

Music 19
  Box 2431
  Rockville, MD 20852
  (Specializes in music games)

Musik Innovations
  9600 Perry Highway
  Pittsburgh, PA 15237

Note-ably Yours
  6865 Scarff Road
  New Carlisle, OH 45344
  (Folk music, books, and records)

Revells Music and Books
  Box 290
  Cambridge, MA 02238

West Music Company
  P. O. Box 5521
  1212 5th Street
  Coralville, IA 52241
  (Music education materials and instruments)

## Music Novelties

Music Treasures Company
  327 Burnwick Road
  Richmond, VA 23227

## Instrument Companies

### Orff Instruments

Golden Bridge, USA
  P. O. Box 24469
  Cleveland, OH 44124

Lyons
    P. O. Box 1003
    Elkhart, IN 46515

Oscar Schmidt International
    230 Lexington Drive
    Buffalo Grove, IL 60089

Sonor Percussion
    HSS
    Lakeridge Industrial Park
    P. O. Box 15035
    Richmond, VA 23227

Studio 49—MMB
    10370 Page Industrial Blvd.
    St. Louis, MO 63132

Suzuki Corporation
    P. O. Box 261030
    San Diego, CA 92126

## Strings

The Luthier Shop
    Route 3, Box 406, Mosley Road
    Aubrey, TX 76227

Lyon and Healy Harps
    168 North Ogden Avenue
    Chicago, IL 60607

Meisel Music, Inc.
    32 Commerce Street
    Springfield, NJ 07081

Shar Products
    P. O. Box 1411
    Ann Arbor, MI 48106

## Woodwinds/Brass

Armstrong Company
    1000 Industrial Parkway
    P. O. Box 787
    Elkhart, IN 46514

Boosey and Hawkes
    200 Smith Street
    Farmingdale, NY 11735

C. G. Conn
    1000 Industrial Parkway
    Elkhart, IN 46516

DEG Music Products
    Highway H North
    Lake Geneva, WI 53147

The Flute Network
    P. O. Box 403
    Cullowhee, NC 28723

Gemeinhardt Company
    P. O. Box 788
    Elkhart, IN 46515

G. Leblanc Corporation
    7019 Thirtieth Avenue
    Kenosha, WI 53141

The Selmer Company
    Box 310
    Elkhart, IN 46515

Frederic Weiner: Musical Instruments
    Sales and Service
    92–16 37th Avenue
    Jackson Heights, NY 11372

The Woodwind and the Brasswind
19880 State Line Rd.
South Bend, IN 46637

## General Instrument Supply

Sam Ash Music Corporation
124 Fulton Avenue
Hempstead, NY 11550

National Music Supply
P. O. Box 14421
St. Petersburg, FL 33733

The Woodwind and Brasswind
50741 U. S. 33 North
South Bend, IN 46637

## Folk/Historical Instruments and Music

American Drum
8440 Barrens Road, N.W.
Roanoke, VA 24019

Antique Sound Workshop
1080 Beacon Street
Brookline, MT 02146

Backyard Music
P. O. Box 9047
New Haven, CT 06532

Kelischek Workshop
Route #1
Brasstown, NC 28902

Lark in the Morning
P. O. Box 1176
Mendocino, CA 95460

Sweet Pipes (recorders and recorder music)
    23 Scholar Lane
    Levittown, NY 11756

Sylvia Woods Music Center (harps and harp music)
    P. O. Box 816
    Montrose, CA 91021

## Percussion

Pearl International
    P O. Box 111240
    Nashville, TN 37222-1240

Purecussion
    5947 West 37th Street
    Minneapolis, MN 55416

## Major Music Houses

Byron Hoyt Sheet Music Service
    2525 Sixteenth Street
    San Francisco, CA 94103-4234

Ted Brown Music Company
    1121 Broadway Plaza
    Tacoma, WA 98402

Educational Affiliates
    8 Newton Plaza
    Plainview, NY 11803

Kidder Music Service
    7623 North Crestline Drive
    Peoria, IL 61615

Malecki Music, Inc.
   4500 Broadmoor SE
   P. O. Box 150
   Grand Rapids, MI 49501

Music Education Center
   3023 Johnson Street
   Hollywood, FL 33021

The Music Mart, Inc.
   210 Yale Boulevard SE
   Albuquerque, NM 87106

PATTI Music Corporation
   414 State Street
   P. O. Box 1514
   Madison, WI 53701

Pender's Music Company
   915 Avenue D
   Denton, TX 76201

Sable's Music Learning Center
   498 Carey Avenue
   Wilkes-Barre, PA 18702

Stanton's Sheet Music, Inc.
   330 South Fourth Street
   Columbus, OH 43215

Jim Starkey Music Center, Inc.
   1318 West Eighteenth Street
   Wichita, KS 67203

Wendell Harrison Music Center
   891 Monroe Avenue
   Rochester, NY 14620

## Electronic and Computer Music Software

Alfred Publishing Co., Inc.
16380 Roscoe Blvd.
P. O. Box 10003
Van Nuys, CA 91410

Sam Ash Music Corporation
124 Fulton Avenue
Hempstead, NY 11550

Coda Music
1401 East 79th
Bloomington, MN 55420

Computers and Music
647 Mission Street
San Francisco, CA 94105

Digital Arts and Technologies
P. O. Box 11, Dept. EME
Milford, CT 06460

Dr. T's Music Software, Inc.
220 Boylston Street, Suite 206
Chestnut Hill, MA 02161

Golden MIDI Music and Software
1020 15th Street, Suite 29K
Denver, CO 80202

Intelligent Music
116 North Lake Avenue
Albany, NY 12206

Maestro Music, Inc.
2403 San Mateo NE, Suite P-12
Albuquerque, NM 87110

Magic Tree
    830 4th Avenue
    Geneva, IL 60134

Music Education Incentives, Inc.
    328E-1 1300 North
    P. O. Box 599
    Chesterton, IN 46304

Swan Software for Arts Education
    P. O. Box 3994
    Eugene, OR 97043

Yamaha Music Corporation, USA
    6600 Orangethorpe Avenue
    Buena Park, CA 90620

# MAJOR COMPOSERS' BIRTHDAYS

| | |
|---|---|
| Johann Sebastian Bach | March 21, 1685 |
| Ludwig van Beethoven | December 16, 1770 |
| Louis Hector Berlioz | December 11, 1803 |
| Johannes Brahms | May 7, 1833 |
| Frederic Chopin | February 22, 1810 |
| Claude-Achille Debussy | August 22, 1862 |
| George F. Handel | February 23, 1685 |
| Franz J. Haydn | March 31, 1732 |
| Franz Liszt | October 22, 1811 |
| Felix Mendelssohn | February 3, 1809 |
| Wolfgang Amadeus Mozart | January 27, 1756 |
| Franz Schubert | January 31, 1797 |
| Robert Schumann | June 8, 1810 |
| Richard Strauss | June 11, 1864 |
| Igor Stravinsky | June 17, 1882 |
| Peter Ilyich Tchaikovsky | May 7, 1840 |
| Giuseppe Verdi | October 10, 1813 |
| Richard Wagner | May 22, 1813 |

# ARTS HISTORY OVERVIEW

An overview of the art, dance, and literature of each music period (covered in chapter 4) is presented. Drama is a form of literature.

## Medieval Period of Music
## (See Time Line 1)

**Major Artists (Carolingian Period, Ottonian Period, Romanesque Art, Gothic Art, early Renaissance)**

Bayeux Tapestry c. 1088

*Painters*

| | |
|---|---|
| Giotto di Bondone | 1266–1336 |
| Duccio di Buoninsegna | 1255–1319 |
| Ambrogio Lorenzetti | 1323–1348 |
| Pietro Lorenzetti | 1305–1348 |
| Simone Martini | 1284–1344 |

*Sculptors*

| | |
|---|---|
| Andrea Pisano | 1290–1350 |

# MEDIEVAL COMPOSERS, ARTISTS, AND AUTHORS 10TH–14TH CENTURIES

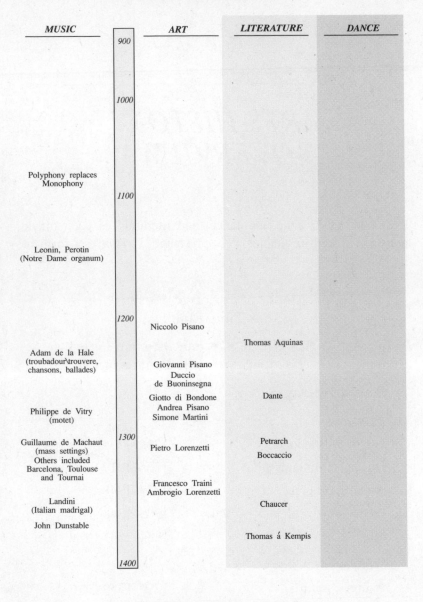

| MUSIC | | ART | LITERATURE | DANCE |
|---|---|---|---|---|
| | *900* | | | |
| | *1000* | | | |
| Polyphony replaces Monophony | *1100* | | | |
| Leonin, Perotin (Notre Dame organum) | | | | |
| | *1200* | Niccolo Pisano | | |
| | | | Thomas Aquinas | |
| Adam de la Hale (troubadour\trouvere, chansons, ballades) | | Giovanni Pisano Duccio de Buoninsegna | | |
| | | Giotto di Bondone Andrea Pisano Simone Martini | Dante | |
| Philippe de Vitry (motet) | | | | |
| Guillaume de Machaut (mass settings) Others included Barcelona, Toulouse and Tournai | *1300* | Pietro Lorenzetti | Petrarch Boccaccio | |
| Landini (Italian madrigal) | | Francesco Traini Ambrogio Lorenzetti | Chaucer | |
| John Dunstable | | | Thomas á Kempis | |
| | *1400* | | | |

*Time Line 1: Medieval Period*

| | |
|---|---|
| Giovanni Pisano | 1250–1317 |
| Niccolo Pisano | 1225–1278 |
| Francesco Traini | 1321–1363 |

*Literature*

| | |
|---|---|
| Thomas Aquinas | 1225–1274 |
| Boccaccio | 1312–1375 |
| Chaucer | c. 1340–1400 |
| Dante | 1265–1321 |
| Thomas á Kempis | 1380–1471 |
| Petrarch | 1304–1374 |

## Renaissance Period of Music
## 15th–16th Centuries
## (See Time Line 2)

**Major Artists**

| | |
|---|---|
| Fra Angelico | 1387–1455 |
| Gentile Bellini | 1426–1507 |
| Giovanni Bellini | 1428–1516 |
| Bosch | 1450–1510 |
| Sandro Botticelli | 1444–1510 |
| Donato Bramante | 1444–1514 |
| Bronzino | 1503–1572 |
| Pieter Bruegel | 1525–1569 |
| Brunelleschi | 1420–1436 |
| Vittore Carpaccio | 1455–1526 |
| Correggio | 1494–1534 |
| Giovanni da Bologna | 1529–1608 |
| Antonello da Messina | 1430–1479 |
| Leonardo da Vinci | 1452–1519 |

## RENAISSANCE COMPOSERS, ARTISTS, AND AUTHORS 15TH–16TH CENTURIES

| *MUSIC* | | *ART* | *LITERATURE* | *DANCE* |
|---|---|---|---|---|
| | *1360* | | | |
| | | Della Quercia | | Court dancing and secular Renaissance forms develop. |
| | *1380* | Lorenzo Ghiberti | | |
| | | Donatello Fra Angelico | | |
| | | Jan van Eyck | | |
| | | Pasolo Uccello | Sir Thomas Malory | |
| Guillaume Dufay | *1400* | Luca della Robbia | | |
| Binchois | | Masaccio | | |
| | | Filippo Lippi | | |
| | *1420* | Domenico Veneziano Piero della Francesca Brunelleschi | | |
| | | Andrea del Castagno | | |
| Johannes de Ockeghem | | Antonio Rossellino | | |
| Jacob Obrecht Heinrich Isaac | | Gentile Bellini Giovanni Bellini Antonello da Messina Andrea Mantegna Andrea del Verrocchio | | |
| | *1440* | | | |
| | | Sandro Botticelli Donato Bramante | | |
| | | Domenico Ghirlandaio Bosch Perugino Leonardo da Vinci | | |
| Josquin des Pres | *1460* | Vittore Carpaccio | | |

Chansons, ballades, virelais, motets, and masses

*Time Line 2: Renaissance Period*

# RENAISSANCE COMPOSERS, ARTISTS, AND AUTHORS 15TH–16TH CENTURIES

| MUSIC | | ART | LITERATURE | DANCE |
|---|---|---|---|---|
| | 1460 | | | |
| | | | Desiderius Erasmus | |
| | | | Machiavelli | |
| | | Matthias Grunewald Albrecht Durer | | |
| | | Michelangelo | | |
| | | Giorgione Jan Gossaert | | |
| | 1480 | | | |
| | | Raphael Sanzio | | |
| | | | Martin Luther | |
| Janequin | | Andrea del Sarto | | |
| | | Correggio Titian | | |
| | | Jacopo Pontormo | | |
| | | Hans Holbein | | |
| | 1500 | | | |
| Gombert | | Francesco Parmigianino Bronzino | | |
| Thomas Tallis | | | | |
| Clemens | | Jean Goujon Giorgio Vasari | | |
| Cipriano de Rore | | Tintoretto | | |
| | 1520 | | | |
| | | Giovanni da Bologna Pieter Bruegel | | |
| Palestrina | | | | |
| | | Paolo Veronese | Montaigne | |
| | 1540 | | | |
| Giovanni Gabrieli Gesualdo John Dowland | 1560 | | Christopher Marlowe William Shakespeare | |
| Claudio Monteverdi | | | | |
| | 1580 | | | The Ballet Comique de la Reize is performed for Catherine de Medici |

*Time Line 2 continued*

| | |
|---|---|
| Andrea del Castagno | 1423–1457 |
| Andrea del Sarto | 1486–1531 |
| Andrea del Verrocchio | 1435–1488 |
| Piero della Francesca | 1420–1492 |
| Luca della Robbia | 1400–1482 |
| Donatello | 1386–1466 |
| Albrecht Dürer | 1471–1528 |
| Lorenzo Ghiberti | 1378–1455 |
| Domenico Ghirlandaio | 1449–1494 |
| Giorgione | 1478–1510 |
| Jan Gossaert | 1478–1535 |
| Jean Goujon | 1510–1565 |
| Matthias Grünewald | 1470–1528 |
| Hans Holbein | 1497–1543 |
| Filippo Lippi | 1406–1469 |
| Andrea Mantegna | 1431–1506 |
| Masaccio | 1401–1428 |
| Michelangelo | 1475–1564 |
| Francesco Parmigianino | 1503–1540 |
| Perugino | 1450–1523 |
| Jacopo Pontormo | 1494–1556 |
| Della Quercia | 1375–1438 |
| Antonio Rossellino | 1427–1479 |
| Raphael Sanzio | 1483–1520 |
| Tintoretto | 1518–1594 |
| Titian | 1490–1576 |
| Paolo Uccello | 1397–1475 |
| Jan van Eyck | 1390–1441 |

| Giorgio Vasari | 1511–1574 |
| Domenico Veneziano | 1420–1461 |
| Paolo Veronese | 1528–1588 |

## Literature

| Desiderius Erasmus | 1466–1536 |
| Martin Luther | 1483–1531 |
| Machiavelli | 1469–1527 |
| Sir Thomas Malory | 1394–1471 |
| Christopher Marlowe | 1564–1593 |
| Montaigne | 1533–1592 |
| William Shakespeare | 1564–1616 |

## Dance

Court dancing and secular Renaissance forms develop. Ballroom dance steps do not differ from theatre dance (that which is performed for audiences).

1581—The Ballet Comique de la Reize is performed for Catherine de Médici.

## Baroque Period of Music
## 17th Century
## (See Time Line 3)

## Major Artists

| Gianlorenzo Bernini | 1598–1680 |
| Annibale Carracci | 1560–1609 |
| Pieter de Hooch | 1629–1683 |
| Georges de la Tour | 1593–1652 |
| José de Ribera | 1591–1652 |

## BAROQUE COMPOSERS, ARTISTS, AND AUTHORS
## 17TH CENTURY

| *MUSIC* | | *ART* | *LITERATURE* | *DANCE* |
|---|---|---|---|---|
| | 1540 | El Greco | Miquel de Cervantes | |
| Jan Sweelinck | 1560 | Annibale Carracoi | Lope de Vega William Shakespeare | |
| Michael Praetorius | | | Ben Johnson John Donne | |
| | | Peter Paul Rubens | | |
| Girolamo Frescobaldi Heinrich Schutz Johann Schein Samuel Scheidt | 1580 | Frans Hals | | |
| | | Gerard Honthorst Jose de Ribera | | |
| | | Georges de la Tour Louis le Nain Nicolas Poussin | | |
| | | Gianlorenzo Bernini Anthony van Dyck Diego de Velazquez Claude Lorrain | Pedro Calderon de la Barca | |
| | 1600 | | | |
| | | Rembrandt | Pierre Corneille | |
| | | | John Milton | |
| | | Bartolome Murillo William Kalf | | |
| | 1620 | | Moliere | |
| | | Jakob van Ruisdael Francois Girardon Pieter de Hooch Jan Steen Jan Vermur van Delft | John Bunyan John Dryden | |
| Jean Baptiste Lully | | | | |
| Dietrich Buxtehude | | | Jean Baptist Racine | |
| | 1640 | | | |

*Time Line 3: Baroque Period*

# BAROQUE COMPOSERS, ARTISTS, AND AUTHORS
## 17TH CENTURY

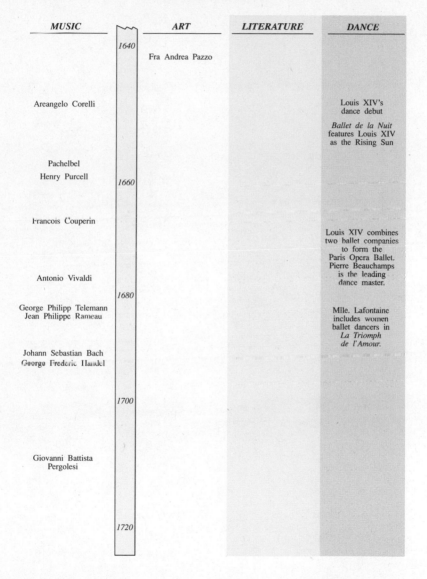

| MUSIC | | ART | LITERATURE | DANCE |
|---|---|---|---|---|
| | *1640* | Fra Andrea Pazzo | | |
| Areangelo Corelli | | | | Louis XIV's dance debut |
| | | | | *Ballet de la Nuit* features Louis XIV as the Rising Sun |
| Pachelbel | | | | |
| Henry Purcell | *1660* | | | |
| François Couperin | | | | Louis XIV combines two ballet companies to form the Paris Opera Ballet. Pierre Beauchamps is the leading dance master. |
| Antonio Vivaldi | | | | |
| | *1680* | | | |
| George Philipp Telemann | | | | Mlle. Lafontaine |
| Jean Philippe Rameau | | | | includes women ballet dancers in *La Triomph de l'Amour.* |
| Johann Sebastian Bach | | | | |
| George Frederic Handel | | | | |
| | *1700* | | | |
| Giovanni Battista Pergolesi | | | | |
| | *1720* | | | |

*Time Line 3 continued*

| François Girardon | 1628–1715 |
| El Greco | 1541–1614 |
| Frans Hals | 1580–1666 |
| Gerard Honthorst | 1590–1656 |
| William Kalf | 1619–1693 |
| Louis le Nain | 1593–1648 |
| Claude Lorrain | 1600–1682 |
| Bartolomé Murillo | 1617–1682 |
| Fra Andrea Pazzo | 1642–1709 |
| Nicolas Poussin | 1594–1665 |
| Rembrandt | 1606–1669 |
| Peter Paul Rubens | 1577–1640 |
| Jan Steen | 1629–1679 |
| Anthony van Dyck | 1599–1641 |
| Jan Vermeer van Delft | 1632–1675 |
| Jakob van Ruisdael | 1628–1682 |
| Diego de Velázquez | 1599–1660 |

## Literature

| John Bunyan | 1628–1688 |
| Miguel de Cervantes | 1547–1616 |
| Pedro Calderón de la Barca | 1600–1681 |
| Lope de Vega | 1562–1635 |
| John Donne | 1573–1631 |
| John Dryden | 1631–1700 |
| Ben Jonson | 1572–1637 |
| John Milton | 1608–1674 |
| Molière | 1622–1673 |
| Pierre Corneille | 1606–1684 |

| Jean Baptist Racine | 1639–1699 |
| William Shakespeare | 1564–1616 |

## Dance

Louis XIII appears in French court ballets. The ballet á entrée (independent scenes on one theme) is popular, marked by variety and display.

1651—Louis XIV makes his dance debut. In 1653 he is the Rising Sun in the *Ballet de la Nuit,* which establishes him as the Sun King.

1661—Louis XIV establishes the Académie Royale de Danse and, in 1669, the Académie Royale de Musique. He combines them in 1672. This is the Paris Opera Ballet, the oldest ballet company in the world. Louis XIV hires Jean Baptist Lully to compose many court ballets. With Molière, Lully creates the Comédie-ballet. Pierre Beauchamps, Louis XIV's teacher, is the leading dance master.

1681—Mlle. Lafontaine includes women ballet dancers in *La Triomph de l'Amour.*

### Classical Period of Music
### 18th Century
### (See Time Line 4)

## Major Artists (Rococo)

| François Boucher | 1703–1770 |
| Jean-Baptiste Siméon Chardin | 1699–1779 |
| Clodion | 1738–1814 |
| Jean Honoré Fragonard | 1732–1806 |
| Thomas Gainsborough | 1727–1788 |
| Jean Baptiste Grueze | 1725–1805 |
| William Hogarth | 1697–1764 |

| Jean Antoine Houdon | 1741–1828 |
| Joshua Reynolds | 1723–1792 |
| Giambattista Tiepolo | 1696–1770 |
| Antoine Watteau | 1684–1721 |

## Literature

| Beaumarchais | 1732–1799 |
| Samuel Coleridge | 1772–1834 |
| Daniel Defoe | 1660–1731 |
| Diderot | 1713–1784 |
| Henry Fielding | 1707–1754 |
| Wolfgang Goethe | 1749–1832 |
| Samuel Johnson | 1709–1784 |
| Metastasio | 1698–1782 |
| Antoine Prévost | 1697–1763 |
| Rousseau | 1712–1778 |
| Sheridan | 1751–1816 |
| Jonathan Swift | 1667–1745 |
| Voltaire | 1694–1778 |

## 18th-Century Dance

Dance moves from the ballroom to the theater and remains an upper-class art form.

The five ballet foot positions become widely used. Ballet *d'action* develops; the form is unified, dramatic, and separate from opera.

1713—The Paris Opera Ballet School opens.

Influential writings are:

    a. Rameau's treatise, *The Dancing Master*.

    b. Noverre's *Letters on Dancing and Ballets*.

# CLASSICAL COMPOSERS, ARTISTS, AND AUTHORS 17TH–18TH CENTURIES

| *MUSIC* | | *ART* | *LITERATURE* | *DANCE* |
|---|---|---|---|---|
| | 1660 | | Daniel Defoe | |
| | | | Jonathan Swift | |
| | 1680 | | | Keeping its upper-class status, dance moves from the ballroom to the theater. |
| | | Antoine Watteau | | |
| Domenico Scarlatti | | | | |
| | | | Voltaire | |
| | | Giambattista Tiepolo | | |
| | | William Hogarth | Antoine Prevost | |
| | | Jean-Baptiste Simeon Chardin | Metastasio | |
| | 1700 | | | |
| G. B. Sammartini | | | | |
| | | Francois Boucher | | |
| | | | Henry Fielding | |
| | | | Samuel Johnson | |
| | | | Rousseau | |
| Christoph Willibald Gluck | | | Diderot | The Paris Opera Ballet School opens. |
| C.P.E. Bach | | | | |
| Johann Stamitz | | | | |
| | 1720 | | | |
| | | Joshua Reynolds | | Five ballet foot positions are popular. |
| | | Jean Baptiste Grueze | | |
| | | Thomas Gainsborough | | |
| A. Soler | | | | |
| Franz Joseph Haydn | | Jean Honore Fragonard | Beaumarchais | |
| Johann Christian Bach | | | | |
| Karl Ditters von Dittersdorf | | Clodion | | |
| | 1740 | Jean Antoine Houdon | | |
| Boccherini | | | | |
| | | | Wolfgang Goethe | |
| | | | Sheridan | |
| Muzio Clementi | | | | |
| W.A. Mozart | | | | |
| Dussek | 1760 | | | |
| Ludwig Van Beethoven | | | Samuel Coleridge | |
| | 1780 | | | |

*Time Line 4: Classical Period*

Diderot employs wires to lift dancers so that they appear to be dancing on their toes.

## Romantic Period of Music
## 19th Century
## (See Time Line 5)

### Artists (Romanticism, Realism, Impressionism, Post-Impressionism)

| | |
|---|---|
| Paul Cézanne | 1839–1906 |
| John Constable | 1776–1837 |
| Jean Baptiste Camille Corot | 1796–1875 |
| Gustave Courbet | 1819–1877 |
| Thomas Couture | 1815–1879 |
| Honoré Daumier | 1808–1879 |
| Jacques Louis David | 1748–1825 |
| Edgar Degas | 1834–1917 |
| Eugène Delacroix | 1798–1863 |
| Paul Gauguin | 1848–1903 |
| Theodore Géricault | 1791–1824 |
| Anne Louis Girodet | 1767–1824 |
| Francisco Goya | 1746–1828 |
| Antoine Jean Gros | 1771–1835 |
| Ingres | 1780–1867 |
| Edouard Manet | 1832–1883 |
| François Millet | 1814–1875 |
| Claude Monet | 1840–1926 |
| Camille Pissarro | 1830–1903 |
| Pierre Renoir | 1841–1919 |
| Auguste Rodin | 1840–1917 |

| | |
|---|---|
| Georges Seurat | 1859–1891 |
| Toulouse-Lautrec | 1864–1901 |
| J. M. W. Turner | 1775–1851 |
| Vincent van Gogh | 1853–1890 |
| James A. McNeill Whistler | 1834–1903 |

## Dance

1820—Carlo Blasis codifies classical ballet techniques in his treatise. Ballet dancing *en pointe* becomes established.

1825—The Moscow (Bolshoi) Ballet is founded.

1841—*Giselle,* the epitome of Romantic ballet, is performed.

1862—Marius Petipa choreographs *The Dancer of Pharaoh* in St. Petersburg.

1870—Saint-Léon choreographs *Coppélia.*

1872—Sergei Diaghilev is born.

1890s—Tchaikovsky's *Sleeping Beauty, The Nutcracker,* and *Swan Lake* are performed under Petipa's leadership in St. Petersburg.

## Literature

| | |
|---|---|
| Louisa May Alcott | 1832–1888 |
| Jane Austen | 1775–1817 |
| William Blake | 1757–1827 |
| Charlotte Brontë | 1816–1855 |
| Emily Brontë | 1818–1848 |
| Elizabeth Barrett Browning | 1806–1861 |
| Robert Browning | 1812–1889 |
| Lord Byron | 1788–1824 |
| Lewis Carroll | 1832–1898 |

# ROMANTIC COMPOSERS, ARTISTS, AND AUTHORS 19TH CENTURY

| MUSIC | | ART | LITERATURE | DANCE |
|---|---|---|---|---|
| | *1740* | | | |
| | | Francisco Goya | | |
| | | Jaques Louis David | | |
| | | | William Blake | |
| | *1760* | | | |
| | | Anne Louis Girodet | | |
| Ludgwig Van Beethoven | | | William Wordsworth | |
| | | Antoine Jean Gros | Walter Scott | |
| | | J. M. W. Turner | Jane Austen | |
| | | John Constable | | |
| Hummel | | | | |
| | *1780* | Ingres | | |
| | | | Stendahl | |
| | | | Washington Irving | |
| Spohr | | | | |
| | | | Lord Byron | |
| | | | James Fennimore | |
| | | Theodore Gericault | Cooper | |
| G. Rossini | | | Percy Bysshe Shelley | |
| | | | John Keats | |
| | | Jean Baptiste | | |
| Franz Peter | | Camille Corot | | |
| Schubert | | | | |
| | | Eugene Delacroix | | |
| | | | Honore de Balzac | |
| | *1800* | | | |
| Hector Berlioz | | | Victor Hugo | |
| Glinka | | | Alexandre Dumas | |
| | | | Ralph Waldo Emerson | |
| | | | George Sand | |
| | | | Nathaniel Hawthorne | |
| | | | Merimic | |
| | | | Elizabeth Barrett Browning | |
| | | | Henry W. Longfellow | |
| Felix Mendelssohn | | Honore Daumier | William Thackeray | |
| Bartholdy | | | Edgar Allan Poe | |
| Robert Schumann | | | Alfred Lord Tennyson | |
| Frederic Chopin | | | Robert Browning | |
| Franz Liszt | | | Charles Dickens | |
| Giuseppi Verdi | | Francois Millet | Herman Melville | |
| Richard Wagner | | | Walt Whitman | |
| Charles Gounod | | Thomas Couture | Charlotte Bronte | Carlo Blasis eadifies |
| Offenbach | | | Emily Bronte | classical ballet |
| | | | George Eliot | techniques in |
| | *1820* | Gustave Courbet | Fedor Dostoevski | *Lais treatise.* |
| | | | Gustave Flaubert | |

*Time Line 5: Romantic Period*

# ROMANTIC COMPOSERS, ARTISTS, AND AUTHORS
## 19TH CENTURY

| *MUSIC* | | *ART* | *LITERATURE* | *DANCE* |
|---|---|---|---|---|
| | 1820 | | | |
| Cesar Franck | | | | |
| Anton Bruckner | | | | Moscow (Bolshoi) |
| Smetana | | | | Ballet founded. |
| | | | Leo Tolstoi | |
| | | | Henrik Ibsen | |
| | | Camille Pissarro | Emily Dickinson | |
| Borodin | | Edward Manet | Lewis Carroll | |
| Johannes Brahms | | James A. Whistler | Louisa May Alcott | |
| | | Edgar Degas | | |
| Camille | | | Mark Twain | |
| Saint-Saens | | | | |
| Georges Bizet | | | | |
| Modest Mussorgshy | | Paul Cezanne | | |
| Peter Ilyich | 1840 | Auguste Rodin | Emile Zola | |
| Tchaikovsky | | Claude Manet | | |
| Antonin Dvorak | | Pierre Renoir | | |
| Edward Grieg | | | S. Mallarme | |
| Rimsky-Korsakov | | | Henry James | |
| *Gabriel Faure* | | | | |
| *Vinunt d'Indy* | | | | |
| | | Paul Gauguin | Huysmans | |
| | | | Guy de Maupassant | |
| | | Vincent van Gogh | Robert Louis | |
| | | | Stevenson | |
| | | | Oscar Wilde | |
| Elgan | | | | |
| Giacomo Puccini | | | | |
| Gustav Mahler | | Georges Seurat | | |
| Hugo Wolf | 1860 | | Anton Chekhov | Marius Petipa |
| Albeniz | | Toulouse-Lautrec | O. Henry | choreographs |
| MacDowell | | | | *The Dancer of* |
| *Glaude Debussy* | | | | *Pharaoh* in |
| Pierne | | | | St. Petersburg |
| Richard Strauss | | | | |
| Jean Sibelius | | | Stephen Crane | Saint-Leon |
| *Paul Dukes* | | | | choreographs |
| *Erik Satie* | | | | Coppelia. |
| Granados | | | | |
| Alexander | | | | Sergei Diaghilev |
| Scrialoin | | | | is born. |
| *Sergei* | | | | |
| *Rachmaninoff* | | | | Petipa leads |
| Reger | | | | Tchaikovsky's |
| *Maurice Ravel* | | | | *Sleeping Beauty,* |
| Respighi | | | | *The Nutcracker,* |
| | 1880 | | | and *Swan Lake* |
| | | | | in performances |
| | 1900 | | | in St. Petersburg. |

French Music Post-Romantic *(Appear in italics)*

*Time Line 5 continued*

| | |
|---|---|
| Anton Chekhov | 1860–1904 |
| James Fennimore Cooper | 1789–1851 |
| Stephen Crane | 1871–1900 |
| Honoré de Balzac | 1799–1850 |
| Guy de Maupassant | 1850–1893 |
| Charles Dickens | 1812–1870 |
| Emily Dickinson | 1830–1886 |
| Fyodor Dostoyevski | 1821–1881 |
| Alexandre Dumas | 1802–1870 |
| George Eliot | 1819–1880 |
| Ralph Waldo Emerson | 1803–1882 |
| Gustave Flaubert | 1821–1880 |
| Nathaniel Hawthorne | 1804–1864 |
| O. Henry | 1862–1910 |
| Victor Hugo | 1802–1885 |
| Huysmans | 1848–1907 |
| Henrik Ibsen | 1828–1906 |
| Washington Irving | 1783–1859 |
| Henry James | 1843–1916 |
| John Keats | 1795–1821 |
| Henry W. Longfellow | 1807–1882 |
| S. Mallarmé | 1842–1898 |
| Herman Melville | 1819–1891 |
| Mérimie | 1803–1870 |
| Edgar Allan Poe | 1809–1849 |
| George Sand | 1804–1876 |
| Walter Scott | 1771–1832 |
| Percy Bysshe Shelley | 1792–1822 |

| | |
|---|---|
| Stendahl | 1783–1842 |
| Robert Louis Stevenson | 1850–1894 |
| Alfred Lord Tennyson | 1809–1892 |
| William Thackeray | 1811–1863 |
| Leo Tolstoi | 1828–1910 |
| Mark Twain | 1835–1910 |
| Walt Whitman | 1819–1892 |
| Oscar Wilde | 1854–1900 |
| William Wordsworth | 1770–1850 |
| Émile Zola | 1840–1902 |

## Twentieth Century Period
### (See Time Line 6)

**Artists (Cubism, Art Nouveau, Expressionism, Dadaism, Surrealism, DeStijl, Futurism, Minimalism)**

| | |
|---|---|
| Georges Braque | 1882–1963 |
| Marc Chagall | 1887–1985 |
| Salvador Dali | 1904–1989 |
| Stuart Davis | 1894–1964 |
| André Derain | 1880–1954 |
| Marcel Duchamp | 1887–1968 |
| Hans Hofmann | 1880–1966 |
| V. Kandinsky | 1866–1944 |
| Paul Klee | 1879–1940 |
| Gustav Klimt | 1862–1918 |
| Franz Kline | 1910–1962 |
| Oscar Kokoschka | 1886–1980 |
| Fernand Léger | 1881–1955 |

| | |
|---|---|
| Aristide Maillol | 1861–1944 |
| Henri Matisse | 1869–1954 |
| Joan Miró | 1893–1983 |
| Piet Mondrian | 1872–1944 |
| Eduard Munch | 1863–1944 |
| Emil Nolde | 1867–1956 |
| Jose Orozco | 1883–1949 |
| Pablo Picasso | 1881–1973 |
| Jackson Pollock | 1912–1956 |
| Mark Rothko | 1903–1973 |
| Georges Rouault | 1871–1958 |
| Gino Severini | 1883–1966 |
| David Alfaro Siqueiros | 1898–1974 |

## Literature

| | |
|---|---|
| Samuel Beckett | 1906-1989 |
| Pearl S. Buck | 1892-1973 |
| Anthony Burgess | 1917– |
| Ray Bradbury | 1920– |
| Jean Cocteau | 1889–1963 |
| Joseph Conrad | 1857–1924 |
| Theodore Dreiser | 1871–1945 |
| T. S. Eliot | 1888–1965 |
| William Faulkner | 1897–1962 |
| F. Scott Fitzgerald | 1896–1940 |
| E. M. Forster | 1879–1970 |
| Robert Frost | 1874–1963 |
| Peter Handke | 1942– |
| Thomas Hardy | 1840–1928 |

| | |
|---|---|
| Ernest Hemingway | 1899–1961 |
| Hermann Hesse | 1877–1962 |
| Aldous Huxley | 1894–1963 |
| James Joyce | 1882–1941 |
| Franz Kafka | 1883–1924 |
| Rudyard Kipling | 1865–1936 |
| D. H. Lawrence | 1885–1930 |
| C. S. Lewis | 1898–1963 |
| Sinclair Lewis | 1885–1951 |
| Jack London | 1876–1916 |
| M. Maeterlinck | 1862–1949 |
| Thomas Mann | 1875–1955 |
| Somerset Maugham | 1874–1965 |
| François Mauriac | 1895–1970 |
| Arthur Miller | 1915– |
| Eugene O'Neill | 1888–1953 |
| George Orwell | 1903–1950 |
| Marcel Proust | 1871–1922 |
| Carl Sandburg | 1878–1967 |
| George Bernard Shaw | 1856–1950 |
| A. Solzhenitsyn | 1918– |
| John Steinbeck | 1902–1968 |
| Henry David Thoreau | 1817–1862 |
| J. R. R. Tolkien | 1892–1973 |
| Thornton Wilder | 1897–1975 |
| Tennessee Williams | 1914–1983 |
| Virginia Woolf | 1882–1941 |
| John Updike | 1932– |
| William Butler Yeats | 1865–1939 |

## TWENTIETH CENTURY COMPOSERS, ARTISTS, AND AUTHORS

| MUSIC | | ART | LITERATURE | DANCE |
|---|---|---|---|---|
| | *1840* | | Thomas Hardy | |
| | | | George Bernard Shaw | |
| | | | Joseph Conrad | |
| Albeniz | *1860* | | | |
| MacDowell | | Aristide Maillol | | |
| | | Gustav Klimt | M. Masterlinck | |
| | | Eduard Munch | | |
| | | | William Butler Yeats | |
| | | | Rudyard Kipling | |
| Granados | | V. Kandinsky | | |
| | | Emil Nolde | | |
| | | Henri Matisse | Marcel Proust | |
| | | Georges Rouault | Theodore Dreiser | |
| Ralph Vaughan Williams | | Piet Mondrian | | |
| Reger | | | Somerset Maugham | |
| Charles Ives | | | Robert Frost | |
| Gustav Holst | | | Thomas Mann | |
| Arnold Schonberg | | | Jack London | |
| | | | Herman Hesse | |
| | | | Carl Sandburg | |
| Respighi | *1880* | | E. M. Forster | |
| | | Paul Klee | | |
| Ernest Bloch | | Andre Derain | | |
| Bela Bartok | | Hans Hofmann | Virginia Woolf | |
| Kodaly | | Fernand Leger | James Joyce | |
| Igor Stravinsky | | Pablo Picasso | Franz Kafka | |
| Edgar Varese | | Georges Braque | D. H. Lawrence | |
| Anton Webern | | Jose Orozco | Sinclair Lewis | |
| Alban Berg | | Gino Severini | T. S. Eliot | |
| | | Oscar Kokoschka | | |
| | | Marcel Duchamp | Eugene O'Neill | |
| Villa-Lobos | | Marc Chagall | | |
| | | | J. R. R. Tolkien | |
| Ibert | | | Pearl S. Buck | |
| Sergei Prokofiev | | Joan Miro | | Martha Graham |
| Darius Milhaud | | Stuart Davis | Aldous Huxley | |
| Arthur Honegger | | | Francois Mauriac | |
| | | | F. Scott Fitzgerald | |
| Piston | | | William Faulkner | |
| Paul Hindemith | | | Thornton Wilder | |
| Howard Hanson | | David Alfaro Siqueiros | C. S. Lewis | |
| Sessions | | | Jean Cocteau | |
| Cowell | | | Ernest Hemingway | |
| George Gershwin | | | | |
| Roy Harris | | | Jean Cocteau | |
| Francis Poulenc | | | Ernest Hemingway | |
| Aaron Copland | *1900* | | | |

*Time Line 6: Twentieth Century Period*

# TWENTIETH CENTURY COMPOSERS, ARTISTS, AND AUTHORS

| MUSIC | | ART | LITERATURE | DANCE |
|---|---|---|---|---|
| | *1900* | | John Steinbeck | |
| Kabalevsky | | Mark Rothko Salvador Dali | | George Balanchine |
| | | | George Orwell | Isadora Duncan establishes dancing school for German children and later tours America. |
| Shostakovich | | | | |
| | | | Samuel Beckett | |
| Carter Olivier Messiaen | | | | |
| Samuel Barber Cage | | Franz Kline Jackson Pollock | | Anna Pavlova performs *The Dying Swan* in St. Petersburg. |
| Benjamin Britten Ginastera Milton Babbitt | | | Tennessee Williams Arthur Miller Anthony Burgess A. Solzhenitsyn | Diaghilev founds **Ballets Russes.** **Denishawn School of Dance** opens in Los Angeles. |
| | *1920* | | Ray Bradbury | |
| | | | | Modern dance taking hold through the efforts of Mary Wigmar, Duncan, Graham, and Denishawn. |
| Pierre Boulez Stockhausen | | | | |
| | | | John Updike | |
| | | | | Balanchine and Kirstein open **School of American Ballet** in New York. |
| | *1940* | | Peter Handke | **American Ballet Theater** is established. |
| | *1960* | | | **New York City Ballet** established in New York State Theatre. |

*Time Line 6 continued*

# Dance

1894—Martha Graham is born

1904—George Balanchine is born

1904—Isadora Duncan establishes dancing school for children in Germany; makes American tour. She bases dance forms on natural body movements, not classical tradition.

1905—Anna Pavlova performs the famous solo, *The Dying Swan,* in St. Petersburg.

1909–1929—Diaghilev founds the contemporary dance company, Ballets Russes. He employs scores by Stravinsky, Prokofiev, Ravel, Debussy, Satie, Strauss, Milhaud, and Poulenc. His famous choreographers include Michel Fokine, Vaslav Nijinsky, Léonide Massine, B. Nijinska, and George Balanchine.

1914—Denishawn (Ted Shawn and Ruth St. Denis) School of Dance opens in Los Angeles.

1920s–1930s—Modern dance takes hold through the efforts of Mary Wigmar, Duncan, Graham, and the Denishawn Company.

1934—George Balanchine and Lincoln Kirstein open School of American Ballet, New York.

1939—The American Ballet Theatre is established.

1944—Premiere of Martha Graham's *Appalachian Spring* (music composed by Aaron Copland).

1957—Balanchine choreographs *Agon.*

1958—Premiere of Martha Graham's *Clytemnestra.*

1964—New York City Ballet established in New York State Theatre.

# *BASIC MUSIC THEORY FOR PARENTS*

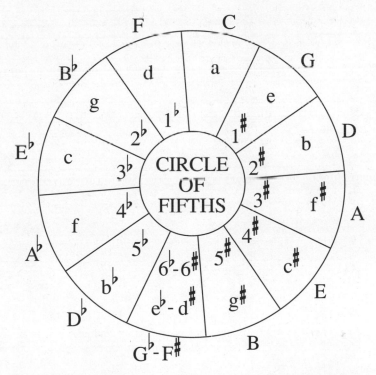

Note: Major keys are indicated by upper case letters and minor keys by lower case letters.

# Examples Using the Key of C

Major Scale:

Natural Minor Scale:

Harmonic Minor Scale:

Melodic Minor Scale:

Intervals:

Chords in Major Scale:

Natural Minor:

Harmonic Minor:

Melodic Minor:

Inversions of a Triad:

Perfect authenic cadence

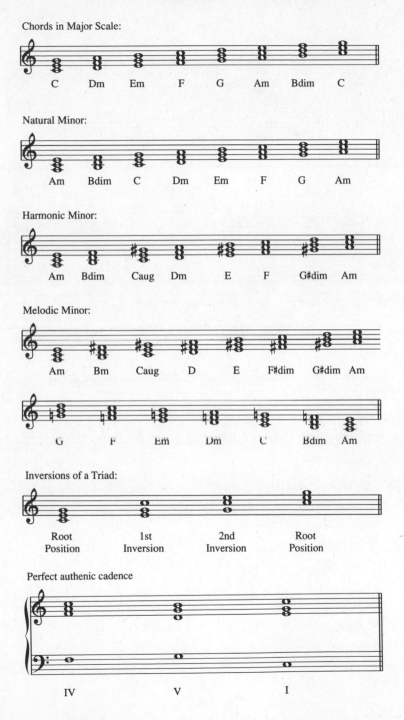

Imperfect authenic cadence

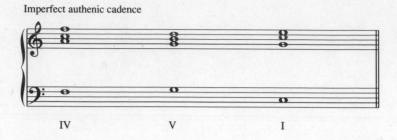

IV                    V                    I

Half cadence

I                    V

Plagal cadence

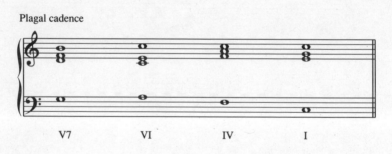

V7          VI          IV          I

# SONGS FOR MUSIC THERAPY AND PASTORAL CARE

## Time to Listen

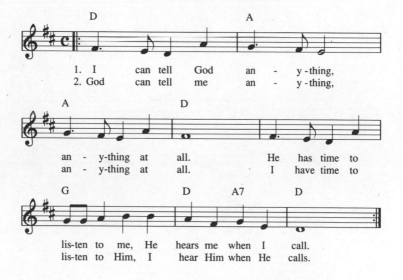

1. I can tell God an-y-thing,
2. God can tell me an-y-thing,

an-y-thing at all. He has time to
an-y-thing at all. I have time to

lis-ten to me, He hears me when I call.
lis-ten to Him, I hear Him when He calls.

## Sometimes I'm Mad

Some-times I'm hap - py, Some-times I'm sad,
Some-times I'm so sweet, Some-times I'm MAD!
So ma-ny feel-ings mixed up in-side, but
I just tell God and His love will guide.

## A Sad Day

When I have a sad day, God gives the best kind of
hugs. His arms nev-er let go, His love nev-er stops. I'm
safe and sound in my Big Dad-dy's lap.

## Talking to My Best Friend

Pray - ing to God, talk - ing to my Best Friend.

Pray - ing to God, let's talk — to God.

## When I'm Afraid

When I'm a - fraid God holds me tight.

He takes a - way all my fright.

---

# PIANO FLUENCY PROGRAM AND IMPROVISATION GUIDE

## Piano Fluency Program

*Student Can Play:*

1. Major scales, 4 octaves through Circle of 5*ths,*

2. Minor scales, 4 octaves through Circle of 5*ths,*

3. Scale variations: in 3*rds,* in 6*ths,* contrary motion, legato/staccato, in different rhythmic pulses, for example:

4. Chromatic scale,

5. Arpeggios

   a. a. on major and minor chords/inversions,

   b. b. 7*ths:* Maj 7, dom 7, min 7, half dim 7, dim 7,

6. The chords in each key and knows all chord types (and inversions):

   a. major,

b. minor,

c. augmented,

d. diminished,

e. 6*ths,*

f. 7*ths*: Major 7, minor 7, dominant 7, half diminished, fully diminished, 9*ths,* 11*ths,* 13*ths,*

7. Suspensions,

8. Trills,

9. Octaves,

10. Finger independence exercises (e.g., double 3*rds* and 6*ths*). (Exercise books help—e.g., Pischna).

*Student Has Background in:*

1. Music theory (harmony, counterpoint, form) and understands figured bass,

2. Ear training, sight singing,

3. Music history beyond own instrument,

4. Introduction to organ, clavichord, harpsichord, etc.,

5. Playing the literature of the following different periods:

## Renaissance:

Fitzwilliam *Virginal Book Collection*

## Baroque:

J. S. Bach

Couperin

Handel

Scarlatti

## Classical:

- C. P. E. Bach
- Beethoven
- Clementi
- Haydn
- Mozart

## Romantic:

- Brahms
- Chopin
- Liszt
- Mendelssohn
- Schubert
- Schumann
- Tchaikovsky

## Post-Romantic/Twentieth Century:

- Bartók
- Debussy
- Fauré
- Gershwin
- Kabalevsky
- Poulenc
- Prokofiev
- Rachmaninoff
- Ravel
- Satie
- Scriabin
- Shostakovitch

Also jazz, rock, folk, ragtime.

# Transposition

*Student can:*

1. Transpose one major key (minor) to another.

2. Modulate to a new key.

3. Transpose major to relative minor and minor to major.

4. Transpose choral warm-ups through keys (C–D♭–D–E♭–E, etc.).

# Improvisation/Composition:

*Student can:*

1. Harmonize a melody.

2. Create a minor rendition.

3. Recognize popular chord notation and can read a lead sheet (melody and chords).

4. Write out a lead sheet.

5. Analyze different music styles and recreate them.

6. Improvise in different styles: jazz, rock, boogie and blues, gospel rock, neoclassic, Baroque, etc.

7. Enjoy creating original music.

8. Write out simple orchestration in score.

*Assignments:*

1. Arrange one song in a variety of styles.

2. Arrange a number of songs in one style (medley).

3. Create an original piece.

4. Orchestrate a composition.

## Accompanying

*Student can:*

1. Sightread fluently

2. Follow another musician's lead

3. Understand the demands of each instrument and how it functions (including voice)

4. Play in ensemble with another pianist (duets, duo works)

5. Accompany a solo voice

*Resource Ideas:*

1. Solo sections from oratorios: e.g., Handel's *Messiah*, Brahms' *Requiem*

2. *Twenty-Four Italian Songs and Arias of the 17th and 18th Centuries* (Schirmer)

3. *Fifty Selected Songs by Schubert, Schumann, Brahms, Wolf, and Strauss* (Schirmer)

4. Fauré—songs: e.g., *Clair de lune*

5. One opera reduction: e.g., Mozart's *Magic Flute*

6. Accompany solo instruments (understands orchestral reduction). Resource Ideas:

    a. Mozart's violin and piano sonata: e.g., K 304

    b. Bach's Sonata No. 1 for flute

    c. Beethoven's cello and piano sonata (No. 2 in G minor. Op. 5)

    d. Handel's *Harp Concerto in B$^b$*

    e. Haydn's *Trumpet Concerto in E$^b$*

    f. Quantz's *Concerto in G for flute*

    g. Debussy's *Violin Sonata in G minor*

    h. Mendelssohn's *Violin Concerto in E minor*

    i. Bloch's *Violin Sonata*

7. Accompany choirs (is familiar with serious, popular, and sacred literature). Recommended works:

   a. Handel's *Messiah*

   b. Bach's *Magnificat*

   c. Mozart's *Requiem*

   d. Brahms' *Requiem*

   e. Verdi's *Requiem*

   f. Mendelssohn's *Elijah*

   g. Stravinsky's *Symphony of Psalms*

8. Play in chamber ensemble (or orchestra). Resource Ideas:

   a. Telemann's *Suite in A minor*

   b. Mozart's *Piano Trio K. 496*

   c. Beethoven's *Piano Trio Op. 97*

   d. Brahms' *Horn Trio, Piano Quintet in F minor*

   e. Schubert's *Quintet in A, Op. 114*

   f. Claude Bolling's *Jazz Suite*

## Score Reading

*Student can:*

1. Read soprano, alto, tenor, bass in hymn/chorale.

2. Read four-part choral score (see choral works for resources).

3. Play different parts in combination (e.g., alto and bass, soprano and tenor, etc.)

4. Read alto and tenor clef and is introduced to orchestral score. Recommended Resources:

   a. Morris and Ferguson. *Preparatory Exercises in Score-Reading.* London: Oxford University Press, 1931.

b. Melcher and Warch. *Music for Score Reading*. Englewood Cliffs, NJ: Prentice-Hall, 1971.

## Improvisation Guide

The following guide is intended for the intermediate/advanced pianist, already comfortable in theory and technique.

### Basics Review

A *lead sheet* has the melody and popular chord symbols. The best investment for a student is a *fake book,* containing hundreds of songs in lead sheet format.

In the following chord overview, popular chord symbols are used above, and figured bass (traditional theory) is shown below.

Students should be comfortable playing these chords in all keys in different inversions and should understand correct voice leading.

Students should practice getting a more contemporary sound by playing the chord in the right hand omitting the root. They should play the octave root in the left hand. Example:

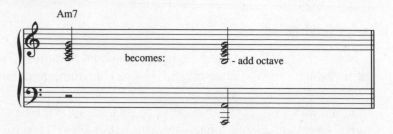

Students should be comfortable transposing from major to minor. Jazz is derived from minor modes. For example *Twinkle Little Star:*

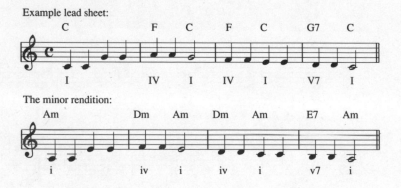

## Improvisation Styles Overview

Once the student is comfortable playing melody and chords from a lead sheet, the fun begins. The joy of improvisation is changing the character of a piece by altering the rhythms and harmonies. We will use well-known folk songs as examples of different styles.

Techniques employed in the following contemporary *Twin-kle* version:

1. Minor and major 7*th* chords are substituted for major tri-ads. The melody note is the 7*th* or 5*th* (can be 3*rd*) of 7*th* chord. Note that roots are omitted from right hand.

2. The beat is syncopated (anticipated), termed "accent dis-placement."

3. The tonic/dominant octave base rhythmically outlines the chord.

4. Clusters (7*ths* with suspensions) are included.

from Collage for Childhood
© Copyright 1989 Mary Ann Froehlich

*Joy to the World* example:

from Collage for Christmas
© Copyright 1989 Mary Ann Froehlich

You are discovering that jazz improvisation is based on mixing minor and major modes. A typical substitute progression is:

The jazz blues scale is:

Note the use of minor intervals: flat 3, 5, and 7. Displaced accents are typical:

The left hand often takes the syncopated rhythm.

An easy way to become comfortable with displaced accents is to practice scales accenting the off-beat:

Triplet rhythms are also typical.

Try playing scales in triplet rhythms: Minor scales sound more "jazzy."

Boogie and blues uses the following left-hand patterns, while the right hand has the syncopated melody.

*Gospel rock* is a derivation of jazz blues. Note the use of the flatted 3*rd* and 5*th* in the following chorus of *Jesus Loves Me:*

Mary Ann Foehlich

Observe that the typical ending is simply triads with the flat
3*rd* and 5*th* traveling down the keyboard.

Compare the gospel version with a more contemporary rendition. Note the use of minor 7, 9 clusters and the arpeggiated
left hand using 7*ths* and 9*ths*.

Cadd2   Bbadd2   Ebadd2   EbMaj9      BbMaj9

from Collage for Worship
© Copyright 1989 Mary Ann Froehlich

Syncopated arpeggios using 7*ths* and 9*ths* in the left hand are also effective.

*Jazz/Rock*

In jazz/rock style *Row Your Boat* evidences:

   a. Driving, constant rhythm.

   b. Displaced accents.

   c. Tonic/dominant octave bass.

   d. The popular sound: triad in right hand, dominant 7*th* in bass: C/Bb

Csus                              C        Dm/C

from Collage for Childhood
© Copyright 1989 Mary Ann Froehlich

*"Neo" styles* are copies of historical styles. For example, neo-Baroque copies the Baroque style. Neo-Classical copies the Classical (e.g., Mozart) style—for example *Twinkle Little Star:*

Techniques of the Classical period are used:

    a. Alberti bass (repeated outlined chords).

    b. Ornamentation, scale figures.

Arranging in "neo" styles requires a knowledge of music history.

Other composition techniques for altering melodies:

Mary Had a Little Lamb: unaltered

Augmentation: double note values

Diminution: cut note values in half

Retrograde: backwards

Inverted: intervals are reversed

Augmentation/Retrograde

Diminution/Inverted

This guide was intended not as a "how to" course but as a concise overview of improvisational techniques: contemporary jazz/rock, gospel rock, boogie/blues, and "neo" styles.

Students learn improvisation from a good model (teacher) and from listening to a variety of styles. My students have enjoyed arranging:

1. One song in a number of styles.

2. Several melodies in one style.

# COLLAGES

- Collage for Childhood*
  (*Twinkle Little Star; Row Your Boat; Go Tell Aunt Rhody; Three Blind Mice; London Bridge, Brahms' Lullaby*)

- Collage for Worship
  (*Jesus Loves Me; My Jesus, I Love Thee; Turn Your Eyes upon Jesus; Sweet, Sweet Spirit; Take My Life and Let It Be*)

- Celebration
  (*Suzuki Vol. I Pieces: Chant Arabe; Christmas Day Secrets*)

- Collage for Christmas I: (Worship)
  (*Joy to the World; Silent Night; What Child Is This?; O Come, Emmanuel; The First Noel; We Three Kings*)

- Collage for Christmas II
  (*Twelve Days of Christmas; Deck the Halls; Jingle Bells; O Christmas Tree; We Wish You a Merry Christmas*)

---

\* All of the collages on this page were authored by Mary Ann Froehlich and are available from F. C. Publishing Co., 309 West 6th Avenue, Ellensburg, WA 98926. (Piano/harp versions)

---

# BIBLICAL REFERENCES TO MUSIC AND DANCE

## Music

**Genesis**

Genesis 4:21
Genesis 31:27

**Exodus**

Exodus 15:1
Exodus 15:2
Exodus 15:21
Exodus 32:18

**Numbers**

Numbers 21:17

**Deuteronomy**

Deuteronomy 31:19
Deuteronomy 31:21
Deuteronomy 31:22
Deuteronomy 31:30
Deuteronomy 32:44

**Judges**

Judges 5:1
Judges 5:3
Judges 5:11
Judges 5:12

**1 Samuel**

1 Samuel 10:5
1 Samuel 16:16
1 Samuel 16:17
1 Samuel 16:18
1 Samuel 16:23
1 Samuel 18:6
1 Samuel 18:7
1 Samuel 18:10
1 Samuel 19:9
1 Samuel 21:11
1 Samuel 29:5

**2 Samuel**

2 Samuel 3:33
2 Samuel 6:5
2 Samuel 19:35
2 Samuel 22:1
2 Samuel 22:50
2 Samuel 23:1

**1 Kings**

1 Kings 1:40
1 Kings 4:32
1 Kings 10:12

**2 Kings**

2 Kings 3:15

**1 Chronicles**

1 Chronicles 6:31
1 Chronicles 6:32
1 Chronicles 6:33
1 Chronicles 9:33
1 Chronicles 13:8
1 Chronicles 15:16
1 Chronicles 15:19
1 Chronicles 15:20
1 Chronicles 15:21
1 Chronicles 15:22
1 Chronicles 15:27
1 Chronicles 15:28
1 Chronicles 16:5
1 Chronicles 16:9
1 Chronicles 16:23
1 Chronicles 16:33
1 Chronicles 16:42
1 Chronicles 23:5
1 Chronicles 25:6
1 Chronicles 25:7

**2 Chronicles**

2 Chronicles 5:12
2 Chronicles 5:13

2 Chronicles 7:6
2 Chronicles 9:11
2 Chronicles 20:21
2 Chronicles 20:22
2 Chronicles 23:13
2 Chronicles 23:18
2 Chronicles 29:26
2 Chronicles 29:27
2 Chronicles 29:28
2 Chronicles 29:30
2 Chronicles 30:21
2 Chronicles 31:2
2 Chronicles 34:12
2 Chronicles 35:15
2 Chronicles 35:25

**Ezra**

Ezra 2:41
Ezra 2:65
Ezra 2:70
Ezra 3:11
Ezra 7:7
Ezra 7:24
Ezra 10:24

**Nehemiah**

Nehemiah 7:1
Nehemiah 7:44
Nehemiah 7:67
Nehemiah 7:73
Nehemiah 10:28
Nehemiah 10:39
Nehemiah 11:22
Nehemiah 11:23
Nehemiah 12:8
Nehemiah 12:27
Nehemiah 12:28
Nehemiah 12:29
Nehemiah 12:36
Nehemiah 12:42
Nehemiah 12:45
Nehemiah 12:46
Nehemiah 12:47
Nehemiah 13:5
Nehemiah 13:10

**Job**

Job 21:12
Job 29:13
Job 30:9
Job 35:10
Job 36:24

Job 38:7

**Psalms**

Psalms 4:1
Psalms 5:1
Psalms 5:11
Psalms 6:1
Psalms 7:1
Psalms 7:17
Psalms 8:1
Psalms 9:1
Psalms 9:2
Psalms 9:11
Psalms 11:1
Psalms 12:1
Psalms 13:1
Psalms 13:6
Psalms 14:1
Psalms 18:1
Psalms 18:49
Psalms 19:1
Psalms 20:1
Psalms 21:1
Psalms 21:13
Psalms 22:1
Psalms 27:6
Psalms 28:7
Psalms 30:1
Psalms 30:4
Psalms 30:12
Psalms 31:1
Psalms 32:7
Psalms 32:11
Psalms 33:1
Psalms 33:2
Psalms 33:3
Psalms 36:1
Psalms 39:1
Psalms 40:1
Psalms 40:3
Psalms 41:1
Psalms 42:1
Psalms 42:8
Psalms 44:1
Psalms 45:1
Psalms 45:8
Psalms 46:1
Psalms 47:1
Psalms 47:6
Psalms 47:7
Psalms 48:1
Psalms 49:1
Psalms 51:1

Psalms 51:14
Psalms 52:1
Psalms 53:1
Psalms 54:1
Psalms 55:1
Psalms 56:1
Psalms 57:1
Psalms 57:7
Psalms 57:9
Psalms 58:1
Psalms 59:1
Psalms 59:16
Psalms 59:17
Psalms 60:1
Psalms 61:1
Psalms 61:8
Psalms 62:1
Psalms 63:5
Psalms 63:7
Psalms 64:1
Psalms 65:1
Psalms 65:8
Psalms 65:13
Psalms 66:1
Psalms 66:2
Psalms 66:4
Psalms 67:1
Psalms 67:4
Psalms 68:1
Psalms 68:4
Psalms 68:6
Psalms 68:25
Psalms 68:32
Psalms 69:1
Psalms 69:12
Psalms 69:30
Psalms 70:1
Psalms 71:22
Psalms 71:23
Psalms 75:1
Psalms 75:9
Psalms 76:1
Psalms 77:1
Psalms 77:6
Psalms 78:63
Psalms 80:1
Psalms 81:1
Psalms 81:2
Psalms 83:1
Psalms 84:1
Psalms 85:1
Psalms 87:1
Psalms 87:7

Psalms 88:1
Psalms 89:1
Psalms 89:12
Psalms 90:14
Psalms 92:1
Psalms 92:3
Psalms 92:4
Psalms 95:1
Psalms 95:2
Psalms 96:1
Psalms 96:2
Psalms 96:12
Psalms 96:13
Psalms 98:1
Psalms 98:4
Psalms 98:5
Psalms 98:8
Psalms 98:9
Psalms 100:2
Psalms 101:1
Psalms 104:12
Psalms 104:33
Psalms 105:2
Psalms 106:12
Psalms 107:22
Psalms 108:1
Psalms 108:3
Psalms 109:1
Psalms 118:14
Psalms 119:54
Psalms 119:172
Psalms 120:1
Psalms 121:1
Psalms 122:1
Psalms 123:1
Psalms 124:1
Psalms 125:1
Psalms 126:1
Psalms 126:2
Psalms 126:5
Psalms 126:6
Psalms 127:1
Psalms 128:1
Psalms 129:1
Psalms 130:1
Psalms 131:1
Psalms 132:1
Psalms 132:9
Psalms 132:16
Psalms 133:1
Psalms 134:1
Psalms 135:3
Psalms 137:3

Psalms 137:4
Psalms 138:1
Psalms 138:5
Psalms 139:1
Psalms 140:1
Psalms 144:9
Psalms 145:7
Psalms 146:2
Psalms 147:1
Psalms 147:7
Psalms 149:1
Psalms 149:3
Psalms 149:5

## Proverbs

Proverbs 25:20
Proverbs 29:6

## Ecclesiastes

Ecclesiastes 2:8
Ecclesiastes 7:5
Ecclesiastes 12:4

## Song of Songs

Song of Songs 1:1
Song of Songs 2:12

## Isaiah

Isaiah 5:1
Isaiah 12:2
Isaiah 12:5
Isaiah 12:6
Isaiah 14:7
Isaiah 16:10
Isaiah 23:15
Isaiah 23:16
Isaiah 24:9
Isaiah 24:16
Isaiah 25:5
Isaiah 26:1
Isaiah 27:2
Isaiah 30:29
Isaiah 30:32
Isaiah 35:10
Isaiah 38:18
Isaiah 38:20
Isaiah 42:10
Isaiah 42:11
Isaiah 44:23
Isaiah 49:13
Isaiah 51:3

Isaiah 51:11
Isaiah 52:9
Isaiah 54:1
Isaiah 55:12
Isaiah 65:14

## Jeremiah

Jeremiah 20:13
Jeremiah 30:19
Jeremiah 31:7

## Lamentations

Lamentations 3:14
Lamentations 3:63
Lamentations 5:14

## Ezekiel

Ezekiel 26:13
Ezekiel 33:32

## Daniel

Daniel 3:5
Daniel 3:7
Daniel 3:10
Daniel 3:15

## Hosea

Hosea 2:15

## Amos

Amos 5:23
Amos 6:5
Amos 8:3
Amos 8:10

## Jonah

Jonah 2:9

## Micah

Micah 2:4

## Habakkuk

Habakkuk 3:19

## Zephaniah

Zephaniah 3:14
Zephaniah 3:17

## Matthew

Matthew 9:23
Matthew 11:17
Matthew 26:30

## Mark

Mark 14:26

## Luke

Luke 7:32
Luke 15:25

## Acts

Acts 16:25

## Romans

Romans 15:9
Romans 15:11

## 1 Corinthians

1 Corinthians 14:7
1 Corinthians 14:15

## Ephesians

Ephesians 5:19

## Colossians

Colossians 3:16

## Hebrews

Hebrews 2:12

## James

James 5:13

## Revelation

Revelation 5:9
Revelation 5:12
Revelation 5:13
Revelation 14:2
Revelation 14:3
Revelation 15:3
Revelation 18:22

# Dance

## Exodus

Exodus 15:20
Exodus 32:19

## Judges

Judges 11:34
Judges 21:21
Judges 21:23

## 1 Samuel

1 Samuel 18:6
1 Samuel 18:7
1 Samuel 21:11
1 Samuel 29:5

## 2 Samuel

2 Samuel 6:14
2 Samuel 6:16

## 1 Kings

1 Kings 18:26

## 1 Chronicles

1 Chronicles 15:29

## Job

Job 21:11

## Psalms

Psalms 30:11
Psalms 149:3
Psalms 150:4

## Ecclesiastes

Ecclesiastes 3:4

## Song

Song of Songs 6:13

## Jeremiah

Jeremiah 31:4
Jeremiah 31:13

## Lamentations

Lamentations 5:15

## Matthew

Matthew 11:17
Matthew 14:6

## Mark

Mark 6:22

## Luke

Luke 7:32
Luke 15:25

# *ABOUT THE AUTHOR*

Mary Ann Froehlich is a Suzuki music educator and Registered Music Therapist-Board Certified trained in Orff-Schulwerk. She holds the D.M.A. in music education/music therapy from the University of Southern Californa, an M.A. in theology from Fuller Theological Seminary, and an M.A. and B.M. in piano and harp performance and music therapy. Mary Ann has worked in hospitals, schools, churches, and private practice and has taught preschool church choirs through university classes. She is a frequent contributor to professional journals and the author of *What's a Smart Woman Like You Doing in a Place Like This?* (Wolgemuth & Hyatt, 1989).

The author has specialized in working with the exceptional and hospitalized. She is a Certified Child Life Specialist and published her doctoral research on the use of music therapy with chronically and terminally ill patients in a children's hospital.

Mary Ann and her husband, John, have three children and live in Benecia, California.

The typeface for the text of this book is *Times Roman*. In 1930, typographer Stanley Morison joined the staff of *The Times* (London) to supervise design of a typeface for the reformatting of this renowned English daily. Morison had overseen type-library reforms at Cambridge University Press in 1925, but this new task would prove a formidable challenge despite a decade of experience in paleography, calligraphy, and typography. *Times New Roman* was credited as coming from Morison's original pencil renderings in the first years of the 1930s, but the typeface went through numerous changes under the scrutiny of a critical committee of dissatisfied *Times* staffers and editors. The resulting typeface, *Times Roman*, has been called the most used, most successful typeface of this century. The design is of enduring value to English and American printers and publishers, who choose the typeface for its readability and economy when run on today's high-speed presses.

*Substantive Editing:*
Michael S. Hyatt

*Copy Editing:*
Donna Sherwood

*Cover Design:*
Steve Diggs & Friends
Nashville, Tennessee

*Page Composition:*
Xerox Ventura Publisher
Printware 720 IQ Laser Printer

*Printing and Binding:*
Maple-Vail Book Manufacturing Group
York, Pennsylvania

*Cover Printing:*
Strine Printing Company
York, Pennsylvania